Cynthia —

Let a muse be your guide,
and a ruse be your device.

— Ken

GEORGE
KRAUSE

A Retrospective

Anne W. Tucker

GEORGE KRAUSE

Rice University Press

Houston, Texas

Edited by Susan Bielstein
Book design by Diane Butler and Associates
Printed and bound in Hong Kong by Dai Nippon
Printing Co., Ltd.

Tucker, Anne.
George Krause/by Anne W. Tucker & George Krause.
    p.   cm.
Includes bibliographical references.
ISBN 0-89263-309-3: $39.95.
1. Photography, Artistic.
2. Krause, George, 1937-   .
I. Krause, George, 1937-   .
II. Title.
TR654.T83 1991
770`.92—dc20   91-52694
CIP

This publication has been made possible through
the generous support of Louisa Stude Sarofim, Ginny
Itz, Harrison Itz, Richard and Janet Caldwell, Frank
and Ana Marie McGinnis, and Harris Gallery. We
are also grateful to the University of Houston for the
limited-grant-in-aid award and to the Cultural Arts
Council of Houston.

Research for the essay was greatly assisted by
George Krause, Sylvia Strenk, Elizabeth Claud, Diane
Brubaker, Joe D. Wheeler, Susan Kismaric, and the
library staff at the Museum of Fine Arts, Houston:
Jeannette Dixon, Margaret Ford, Honey Harrison,
and Marty Stein.

For my mother
-George Krause

For Joe
-Anne W. Tucker

A neatly dressed, middle-aged woman in a cloth coat walked through George Krause's exhibition in February 1978. Sixty prints were on view in two galleries at the Museum of Fine Arts, Houston. The first room featured photographs of Catholic statuary from Krause's series titled Saints and Martyrs. The next gallery exhibited prints from his series I Nudi. Without comment, the woman studied the often tortured religious figures pictured in the first room and then proceeded down the wall of nudes in the second gallery. In the fifth nude print, Krause had photographed a straight beam of light falling across the floor and onto a woman's body, between her extended legs, portraying how he imagined the Greek deity Zeus would ravish a mortal female while disguised as a ray of light. Muttering that no one but a midwife was supposed to see "that," the viewer marched out of the galleries. During the same exhibition, a nurse called the museum's curator to state that she "didn't come to museums to see hairy penises," but rather expected to find only objects of beauty.[1]

Images of nudity are frequent sources of contention between artists and the general public. Nakedness is as ordinary in art as it is in medicine, but its occurrence in art continues to cause public discomfort because art is displayed in public and may be viewed in the presence of strangers, instantly exposing one's responses. Krause joins a long list of distinguished artists to land afoul of "community standards." The most recent additions are, of course, photographers Robert Mapplethorpe and Andres Serrano, performance artist Holly Hughes, and painter Mike Kelley.

But the nineteenth-century struggles of another Philadelphian seem more pertinent to understanding Krause's work. In 1886 Thomas Eakins' life-drawing class was abruptly canceled by the Pennsylvania Academy of Fine Arts when, in a carefully preannounced lecture on the pelvic region delivered to both male and female students, Eakins removed a loincloth from a male model to demonstrate the origin of a muscle. Eakins had scrupulous notions about the necessity of the exact rendition, eschewing affectation, flattery, and stylized representation. He thought the naked human body the most beautiful thing in nature and that "respectability in art is appalling."[2]

In an 1877 article entitled "Art?" an unsigned critic argued that Eakins' own standards must be secondary to those of polite society. The views expressed in this article and another critique by Philadelphian James Whitney echo in spirit, if not in language, articles printed in America in 1990. Whitney wrote:

"To paint well the human figure, models are necessary, . . . but we deny that to paint the human figure utterly naked is to paint it well. And to paint it in any condition of exposure that lowers our sense of the dignity of the human being should be forbidden by directors of life-schools. . . . Because public opinion elsewhere tolerates the hiring of female models, shall we debase our standard to the same level? Because a painter—we cannot say artist—chooses to sit for hours to depict a naked woman of purchased presence, and—to make the occupation both prof-

itable and respectable—sends to a public gallery his shameless copy, have men who are gentlemen and delicate-minded ladies whom the law defends from some other public indecencies, no protection?"[3]

Eakins and Krause are strikingly similar in their inability to temper their conception of art to others' moral standards. Neither man lacks moral scruples, but as the painter Fairfield Porter wrote of Eakins, "The rhetoric he despised was inapplicable to the world he both accepted and chose."[4] Porter continued, "He tried to make art acceptable to himself by the thoroughness of his learning and his practical skills. And so he puts the burden of disproof on the spectator whom he challenges to find that this art, expressing the spectator's disbelief in art, is not valid. If he can make an art for those who care nothing for it . . . what objections can they possibly have."[5]

Following Porter's reasoning, Krause and Eakins also share a capacity for seemingly sincere surprise at each instance of public outrage. Krause, like Eakins, isn't trying to offend his audience. "I like pulling the rug out, throwing people off balance," he says, "but I don't like the idea of a sensational confrontation. I don't want to offend. It is too easy to offend. I don't see any value in that. If someone finds the work offensive, I will sit and talk with them. At times, I have even taken an image out of an exhibition. But it is one of the most wonderful things for an artist to be part of someone's experience when they do find redeeming value in the work."[6]

He does want viewers to confront—as he has—certain basic emotional issues common to humanity. For thirty years he has addressed the topics of sensuality, spirituality, and death among other less-provocative, if not less-crucial, matters. However satisfied others might be to avoid potentially disturbing subjects, Krause perceives dead-on confrontations vital to his evolution as a man and an artist. Critic Patricia Johnson realized that his photographs were "born out of Krause's need to study, analyze and express his fantasies and emotions. They speak directly to the viewer through his or her nerve endings and that is exactly what he wants them to do."7 As a perceptive student reviewer at the University of New Mexico ascertained, "Krause manages to say something about the reality of being human. And by saying that something, we are able to feel a little more aware of our own humanity and the humanity of others, although we may not care to be so brutally enlightened. Krause does not try to soften the blow when the reality impacts. Rather he implodes it with a sort of fantastic wryness, catching images just at the elusive junction of what is real and what isn't."8

Krause does not strike one as a radical. His appearance is conventional in the casual style of his working-class origins. Physically fit, he plays football on Sunday afternoons and prides himself on outplaying younger men. He has a jovial manner that belies a natural shyness. When engaged in conversation, his enthusiasm for certain subjects bubbles forth in a stream of incomplete sentences. Passionate interests include sports, classical music, Japanese and Italian films, and Spanish painters from El Greco to Zurbarán. He lives simply in a two-story garage converted in large part by his own hand. His son, George Krause, Jr., a sculptor and professional carpenter, lives nearby; his daughter, Katy, lives next door.

George Krause is the only child of a Pennsylvania German father and a Russian Jewish mother, both of whom were amateur artists. Widowed young, George's mother nurtured her son's innate gifts as a draftsman. A disciplinarian, she believed drawing involved training as well as inborn talent. If George's drawing didn't satisfactorily depict something, he had to redo it. This early emphasis on technique notably contributed to Krause's well-earned reputation later as a master craftsman.

In the early sixties, another woman helped further hone his attitude toward craft. According to Krause, "Ramona Javitz, who headed the picture collection at the Forty-second Street branch of the New York Public Library, made me print over and over again when I was selling her photographs for five dollars each. Since I also had to travel from Philadelphia to New York to deliver them, it was a losing proposition. People were already talking about my precision technique, but she knew there was more in the negatives. A couple of photographs I must have reprinted at least five different times. She would look at them very carefully and say, 'I like these five, but I want you to print

them over again.' I'd come back a week later with five new prints and she'd say, 'I'll accept this one, but these four aren't good enough.' I'd go back and she'd say, 'I'll take this one, but these you're going to have to do again.'"

Master photographer Paul Strand was another influence as taught by disciples Walter Rosenblum and Murray Weiss. Strand used a German printing paper called Leonar, which had slightly pinkish tones instead of the blue-black tones of more popular photographic papers. With those tones in mind, Krause evolved his own print-developing process. After the photograph is bathed in a weak selenium toning solution, it is "burned" with a mixture of potassium ferrocyanide and potassium bromide to give it a pinkish cast. Hues shift according to the tonal density of the image being printed and Krause's intentions.

Krause believes there is no definitive way to print a negative. He likes Ansel Adams' analogy comparing a photographic negative to a musical score open to many interpretations. It may take him years to print from a negative to his satisfaction. "It's not so much a matter of perfecting a craft as a knowledge of oneself," he told gallery owner Paul Cava.9 In printing he aims to recall fully why he took the picture and to realize all of the negative's potential for emotional and visual impact.

Like most photographers he dreads the boredom of reprinting older negatives and tolerates the task by continually challenging himself to push his understanding "one step further." Among the prints that have changed markedly over several decades is *Birds* (Mexico, 1965, page 4). In early prints, the flitting birds appear to be chattering on their perches. It's an appealing, delicately shaded, restless community. Viewing the print, one can understand how singing birds came to symbolize amorous yearnings, and a melodious bird in a cage to denote a kept woman. These birds might suggest preening prostitutes awaiting customers.

In recent versions of the negative (page 31), fewer birds emerge into view. Pale birds appear to be of whitened marble sculpted from darker stone. No longer flighty, they seem imprisoned in their poses. Krause's interpretation has changed from an apparently direct impression of a gentle scene to something portentous. One possible understanding of the new print derives from the traditional role of birds in religious symbolism as winged souls.10 Here the birds are contained, like earthbound souls.

On a more secular note, there is the Mother Goose nursery rhyme:

There were two birds sat on a stone,
One flew away, and then there was one,
The other flew after, and then there was none,
And so the poor stone was left all alone.[11]

In the newer print, certain birds slip into darkness; colony members are gradually isolated. Their flight is not into freedom, but, seemingly, into death. Krause's technical skill is such that the blackness has the shimmering, enveloping quality of night, not the weight and density of earth.

Having attended a vocational high school, Krause attended Philadelphia College of Art (PCA) on a Board of Education scholarship between 1954 and 1957. PCA was then in transition from an archaic program where students studied primarily from plaster casts to more vigorous teaching methods. The new program featured both commercial and fine arts classes, and Krause studied every medium offered—painting, sculpture, printmaking, drawing, and photography.

Intending to become a commercial artist, he concentrated on the graphic arts in his second and third years and was proficient enough in lithography to win a school prize. He also helped PCA professor Jerome Kaplan teach an evening lithography class at Fleisher Art Memorial. During his junior year, someone on the PCA faculty recommended Krause to teach painting and drawing one evening a week at Swarthmore College. "I was terrified," he remembers, "and swore that I'd never teach again." Photography was then only offered at PCA as an adjunct tool for commercial arts, but John Condax, who taught Fundamental Photography, had an infectious enthusiasm for the subject and was another strong influence.

In 1957 Krause decided to postpone his final year in school and enlisted in the army. Photographer Mark Power met Krause in army radio school at Fort Jackson, South Carolina, and has humorously described their experience. "We thought we were enrolled in a graduate course of Advanced Cunning," Power wrote, "learning lessons of subterfuge and deviousness that were to stand us in good stead for the rest of our lives. In our various ways we learned well…George by repeatedly flunking every army course that didn't appeal to him until finally, in desperation, they placed him in intelligence where he remained for the duration of his army career doing absolutely nothing except for important things like meeting his wife and developing his talent."[12]

Another important service the army provided was to drive Krause further away from the career he had anticipated in advertising. Between commercial art and the military, he saw too many negative parallels in the effects of boredom, meanness, and artificial hierarchies. While in the army, he read voraciously and became a film enthusiast. His army duties were minimal; he lived off base and had an air-conditioned darkroom with unlimited access to film and paper.

Fascinated by the racially segregated communities in South Carolina, he became the "picture man" in black neighborhoods. The children played under the porches of raised, shotgun-style cottages, and Krause loved photographing them as they emerged in the glaring sun, and then immersed themselves in the dense shadows. Though few of these pictures remain in Krause's portfolio today, *Scar*, taken in Philadelphia in 1960 (page 37), mirrors the earlier images. The boy's face fills the frame. While his forehead, nose, and lips shine in raking light, his eyes are shadowed, like slits in a tribal mask. The prominent scar across his nose individuates his otherwise impenetrable countenance.

Krause returned to this motif a decade later when he photographed a black child playing in a fountain, *Fountainhead* (Philadelphia, 1970, page i). Again, a live figure is rendered inanimate. The picture is disturbing because the face resembles a death mask. For this reason, it was rejected by the Philadelphia Arts Council, which had commissioned it for a bicentennial poster. Subsequent audiences more readily accepted the picture as a simultaneous record of something morbid and of a child relishing the cool, sensual pleasure of flowing water. "In all its oozing joy," wrote critic Nessa Forman, "the child appears imprisoned, like some Egyptian mummy bound eternally by a thin sheet of water. . . . Real life for Krause can be a dream world where flesh turns to stone."[13]

In 1959, when Krause returned from the army to PCA, it had become an accredited college requiring more than a year's worth of humanities courses before he could graduate. Krause decided to use the remaining year of his scholarship to study filmmaking, photography, printmaking, and drawing without seeking a degree.

During that year, he joined a discussion group descended from the Photo League, a documentary photography organization that existed in New York City between 1936 and 1951.[14] Ex-members of the Photo League and their students and friends met monthly in each others' homes in Brooklyn. The group included photographers Walter Rosenblum, Jack Lessinger, Barney Cole, and Leo Goldstein. Krause and other PCA students drove to New York City with Sol Libsohn or Murray Weiss, two photography instructors who had joined PCA's faculty while Krause was in the army. Libsohn had been a founding member of the Photo League; Weiss was a student of Rosenblum's at Brooklyn College.

Krause remembers this as a unique group that was of enormous importance to young photographers. The critique sessions offered invaluable feedback as well as an impetus to produce new work for each meeting. While Krause had seen some original photographs in the collection of the Philadelphia Museum of Art, the exposure to original prints, particularly those by Paul Strand,

from members' collections increased the educational value of the discussion group.[15] He attended their meetings on and off for four years.

The group's primary interest was in social documentary photography as practiced by Strand, Lewis Hine, the Farm Security Administration photographers, and other mentors of the Photo League. In the early sixties, photographers motivated by social politics were still dominant figures. Edward Steichen's blockbuster exhibition "The Family of Man" was still touring the world five years after its opening at the Museum of Modern Art, and its accompanying book continued to break art-book sales records. Krause's work continued to reflect this documentary orientation. Mostly his portfolio featured images of children playing in urban settings, with a heavy emphasis on outdoor portraiture.

Writing about Krause's early work for an issue of *Contemporary Photographer*, Murray Weiss emphasized the social content of his pictures and praised his straightforward approach, which lacked "the all too common blurred image, the out of focus 'effect,' the unusual angle, the shock-bizarre eye catcher or the technique studded photograph."[16] Weiss declared that "George's touchstone is people. In the virile, sensuous face of a turbanned Negro youth, his many fine photographs of trusting, courageous or shy children or the gestures of a bent, Orthodox Jew and a strolling skid row inhabitant of a bleak cement world, Krause speaks passionately of the artist's deep-rooted love and sympathy for man's hopes and despair."

Krause enjoyed considerable early success with these pictures. Edward Steichen purchased one for the Museum of Modern Art, and in 1963 *Art in America* selected Krause as the only photographer for its annual "Young Talent USA," which also included artists Marisol and James Rosenquist. But social commentary was no longer satisfying. In his artist's statement for *Art in America*, he declared that he planned "to explore the idea of fantasy with the medium of photography."[17]

Henceforth, he sought images rich with interpretations beyond their social import, and began to reject many of his early images, even those that were widely published. Of the nineteen photographs published in *Contemporary Photographer* in 1962, only nine were included in Krause's 1972 monograph. Only three remain in his portfolio and are included in this book: *Stairs* (Columbia, South Carolina, 1961, page 25), *Angel and Cherub* (Philadelphia, 1962, page 44), and *Scar*. All three defy easy assessment. For instance, in *Angel and Cherub*, an angel kneels and prays while a cherub proclaims through screened windows with peeling-paint frames in an otherwise elegant building. "Angel" comes from the Greek word *angelos*, meaning "messenger." Are these immaterial beings signifying a moment of "grace" in this abode? Or perhaps this is the Archangel Gabriel here to intervene in the affairs of mankind? Only an unimaginative mind would argue that these angels are merely commercial displays in an antique store.

With Murray Weiss and Sol Libsohn, Krause also traveled to Maine in 1963 to meet Berenice Abbott. Krause remembers that Miss Abbott enlisted his help in constructing something for one of her scientific photographs. He was amazed at how inept she was with her hands, while skillful at getting others to do her bidding. Most of the time, he photographed while his companions talked with Abbott. Krause's *White Horse* (page 42) records a white stallion rolling in grass to rid himself of swarms of black flies, which were particularly vindictive that summer. The photograph confirms that Krause was becoming increasingly adept at making complex pictures while not abandoning his straightforward approach. To accept literalism in his work is not wrong, just being satisfied with too little.

The haunting nature of *White Horse* emerges from the graceful torque of the horse's body, its isolation in the lush field, its atypical—and, for a horse, potentially alarming—repose on its side, and its ethereal whiteness against the dark grasses. The last quality has been heightened over years of subtly shifting print tones. A horse is a fecund cultural symbol.[18] In ancient mythology, horses symbolize a journey of the soul, usually to the Other World. Heroes ride horses to win immortality. A saddled but riderless horse is a potent omen. In German, Welsh, and English folklore, to dream of a white horse portends death. Asked about this particular legend, Krause remembers as a young child seeing

a Swedish film in which the passage of a white horse through a village foretells a death, but his conscious thought while photographing the reclining horse was of birth, not death: the city boy thought the snorting stallion was a pregnant mare about to foal. Janus-faced interpretations of birth and death coalesce here in an atmosphere of impending menace. As one critic observed, "Squeezed into the top half of the frame, the kinetic beast has little room to rise."[19] The handsome and powerful body inexplicably reclining creates a seductive and memorable image.

While in the army, Krause had met Pat Johnson, his future wife, who was studying creative writing at the University of South Carolina. After his stint in the army, they moved back to Philadelphia, and in April 1960, George Krause, Jr., was born. George, Sr., supported his family with various freelance jobs. During his fourth year in school, he worked as a graphic artist for Philadelphia designer Samuel Maitin and as a photography assistant for photographer Seymour Mednick. Later he did lettering and mechanicals for the telephone company's Yellow Pages. The job was boring, but Krause liked the flexible schedule. He would work for a straight twenty-four or thirty-six hours and have four or five days free for photography. "It was not a bad way for a young artist to live," says Krause. "I liked working nights and saving days for my own work."

The fall after George, Jr., was born, the family took off, "looking for El Dorado." Traveling by train and bus, their money took them as far as San Francisco. Through a friend, Krause got a job in Utah, but had to wait several months for it to be confirmed. While waiting, he discovered an Italian cemetery across the bay from San Francisco in Daly City where he began to photograph every day.

Krause isn't the first person to respond to a child's birth by focusing on death. It was, however, an enhanced rather than a new preoccupation. His father had died at age twenty-five when Krause was only two, and he grew up wondering about the man he could not remember and fantasizing how his own life might have been different had his father lived. His mother told him he was just like his father, with the unfortunate consequence that Krause began to fear he would also die when he was twenty-five. He believed that he had only five years to live when he began to photograph at age twenty and reached his twenty-sixth birthday with great relief. But when he called his mother to share in his celebration, she countered that she might have been mistaken. His father might have died at twenty-seven.

Krause loves to tell this story, and breaks into hearty laughter with the punch line. He also admits knowing from the moment of his mother's response that he was destined to continue working on his cemetery series. In fact, the series, titled *Qui Riposa*, contains more than two thousand images and is his largest and most actively expanding series, while the other series he began in the fifties, *The Street*, is practically moribund. "I don't walk streets anymore," he acknowledged in 1990. "In the street you could die of hunger. There have been weeks when I've walked the streets and never taken a photograph—whereas I can't imagine working in the cemetery for three hours and not photographing." He adds, "For the kind of aimless walking required for the street series, you need to be young, and have good knees."

Krause first noticed photo-sensitized tiles in Italian cemeteries in Philadelphia. Before traveling to San Francisco, he photographed a baby's tombstone on which a photograph of the infant in its coffin was mounted between the inscription and a weather-worn lamb sculpted at the crest of the headstone (page 7). The picture is saved from sentimentality by the relentless clarity of the death portrait.

In the Daly City graveyard, he was overwhelmed by tombstone photographs. He realized that family histories and relationships were often more intimately revealed by the pictures chosen than by the graves' inscriptions. "Some tombstones reflected great love," he noted. "Others indifference. Some even hate. This was so beautiful and it seemed to me that no one had ever seen them this way. I became involved with the idea of memories, with the imagined lives of the people who were buried under the stones. A woman in her bridal gown, a little girl on roller skates, a cowboy ready to draw. These were photographs selected by relatives of the deceased for definite reasons, each one mirroring an attitude....It was wonderful to be there....I found it to be a peaceful place and started to overcome my fear of death."[20]

Photographing tombstones, Krause particularly notices how attempts to preserve memory are undermined. Time, weather, and vandals have eroded efforts at immortality, and the monuments' deterioration affirms, rather than denies, corruption below. Several critics have found a correspondence between Krause's reach for immortality through art and the thwarted efforts by families of the deceased. A.D. Coleman realized that to see tombstone portraits "gradually solarizing or being eaten away by the weather is to witness the final disappearance of the spirits with which they are invested. In these, particularly, Krause seems to be scourging himself with the impermanence of his own medium and, implicitly, of his own work as well."[21] Critic Caroline Meline similarly noted that a "dark joke contains the central paradox of George Krause's vision, and he knows it is a joke on him, too. Humans erect monuments, but humans must die. Humans create, but what they create are tombstones to celebrate their own deaths. Whatever artistic and spiritual heights we may aspire to or reach, ultimately we are mortal and cannot control our own fates."[22]

Sometimes Krause employs humor—both whimsical and grim—to confront death. In *Juggler* (Italy, 1985, page 119), a statue of Christ appears animated. On the wall behind the statue, hovering above its open palms, glazed oval portraits resemble bubbles, or souls rising on Judgment Day. On a darker note, *Winter* (New York, 1970, page 122) generally causes viewers to either gasp or giggle. Bare branches, resembling roots, appear to sprout from a statue's skull.

Breast (Italy, 1988, page 117) introduces sensuality to the series. Passers-by have rubbed a statue's breast until it shines. The desire to touch is such a powerful, natural impulse that when touching is suggested by the example of others, the invitation is irresistible. On public statues, feet, hands, or knees are commonly worn away by touching, but usually no one strokes a body's intimate parts. In this case, the lure to caress mingles with the titillation of doing something forbidden. One imagines visitors to the cemetery looking over both shoulders before reaching out to the smooth, inviting surface.

For thirty years, Krause has photographed cemeteries in North and South America, Italy, and Spain. He revisits certain sites noting additional names and images on specific family markers as well as trends in gravestone design. Like neighborhoods acceding to the same fence salesman, cemeteries feature repeated examples of the same angel or reliefs based on the same famous painting. After World War II, electricity brought a boom in "eternal" lights, most of which have since burned out. Modern tastes and the desire for low maintenance streamlined tombs' surfaces.

Events in Krause's own life often direct his attention to graves he has previously overlooked. The death of a friend's infant son caused him to focus on children's graves, of which five are illustrated here (pages 7, 15, 109, 121, and 116). Four of the graves recall the child with a snapshot. One infant's face in a heart-shaped frame is a heart-stopping ornament dangling from a Christmas poinsettia. Like provisions left for a pharaoh, a wooden horse and a teddy bear nestle in the flower's leaves. Another child sleeps eternally midst a symbol of paradise, stars and a crescent moon.

Father's Finger (Italy, 1980, page 116) echoes a photograph Krause made in South Carolina in 1958 and has since rejected (page 9). In the earlier picture, a black infant in a dazzling diaper sits on splintered wooden steps, steadied by a firm hand on a disembodied arm. Lacking tenderness, the adult's clasp secures the child's posture without soothing his palpable anxiety. As art, the picture lacks resonance; the viewer's emotions are singularly directed toward a vague sympathy for the cuddly, but apprehensive, child. Twenty years later, Krause discovered a memorial snapshot in which an adult's disembodied hand and a child are similarly linked. Here, an elfin girl grips a guardian's finger tip; her dark eyes peer upward, shyly inquisitive. When initially taken, the Italian snapshot was probably as appealing as any other child's picture—including Krause's from South Carolina. Transformed by its context, it now exudes pathos, compelling us to

grieve for the child and her bereaved family. The ministering angel and flowers caressing her picture provoke a plethora of complex emotions and questions about untimely deaths.

For Krause, the *Qui Riposa* series is also an opportunity to pay homage to journeyman photographers whose unsigned pictures on tombstones offer a mini-history of family portraiture. Many of the pictures were made for special occasions, including yearbooks, military inductions, and passports. Taken in studios, they are pictures for which one dressed well and posed earnestly. Since World War II, families have frequently used snapshots, choosing to remember more casual moments. The sparkle of life arrested in amateurs' pictures contrasts sharply with their graven stone settings.

The introduction of color photographs on gravestones has prompted Krause to occasionally work with color film. He responds to the artificially vivid colors of plastic flowers, neon lights, and inlaid marble—and especially to memorials that depend on color for their impact. In *Red Eyeglasses* (California, 1987, page 132), the woman is not a great beauty. Who wished to remember her in this coy Hollywood pose, feather wrap, flashy glasses, and red lips? The pose and costume are silly, touching, and inappropriate in this context.

Some picture combinations on gravestones present unwitting incongruities. For example, the ancient visage of a widow who outlived her husband by many decades is mounted next to a representation of her long-departed, youthful groom (page 118). While the inscribed dates on the stone reveal fifty-two years of widowhood, the picture alone infers a mother-son relationship. In another example of naive construction, two favorite snapshots were merged without removing the half face-and-body of one person and partial torso of another in the two backgrounds, yielding a ghostly cyclops and vague, floating heart behind the couple (page 112). According to Joseph Campbell, an eye in the middle of the forehead "opens in man...the vision of eternity," so perhaps this fortuitous mistake was advantageous to the couple in the foreground.[23] Krause found more intentional references to the link between open eyes and eternity when the eyes of a corpse were painted eternally open on a tombstone photograph (page 112).

Sometimes, the original intentions of the family are difficult to discern. For instance, in *Foursome* (Italy, 1987, page 108), what was meant by including a drawing of Christ in the frame with photographs of three stolid family members? Contrary to the tradition of presenting Christ as larger than life, the family portraits and the image of Christ are all the same size. And rather than being elevated, Christ is relegated to the lower right-hand corner of the grouping. If the remembrance was intended to be reverent, the results are ambiguous.

Krause worked nine months in Brigham City, Utah, before returning to Philadelphia in 1962. Employed briefly as an assistant to advertising photographer Dan Moerder, he decided not to continue studio work, "applying glycerine to tires and dropping tears on models' faces." He resumed his work as a paste-up artist to support his family, and continued to photograph for himself.

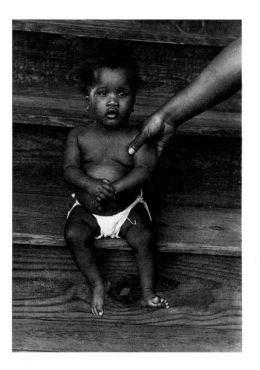

Shortly after Krause returned from Utah, he met John Szarkowski who had recently assumed the directorship of the Museum of Modern Art's photography department. When Steichen purchased a photograph from Krause in 1960, he paid his standard "five dollars a print."[24] Szarkowski purchased seven additional photographs, raising the payment to twenty-five dollars per print. Krause regards the increase as "the biggest thing Szarkowski did that first year."

Szarkowski included Krause in the 1963 exhibition "Five Unrelated Photographers" with Garry Winogrand, Ken Heyman, Jerry Liebling, and Minor White, and that same year, Nathan Lyons, assistant director of the George Eastman House in Rochester, New York, showed his work in two exhibitions: "Three Photographers" (with Carl Chiarenza and Jack Stuler) and "Photography 63/An International Exhibition." In 1964, Szarkowski selected a Krause print from *Qui Riposa* for the seminal exhibition (and book) "The Photographer's Eye," and Lyons included him in "Contemporary Photographers 1," an exhibition that toured the United States until 1970.[25] Throughout the sixties, Szarkowski continued to include Krause's work in exhibitions and articles on contemporary photography. In a 1968 piece titled "The Art of Photography: A Contradiction in Terms?" Szarkowski reproduced one photograph each by Diane Arbus, Garry Winogrand, Minor White, Jerry Uelsmann, Hilmar Pabel, A.L. Syed, and Martin A. Paternotte—and two each by Krause and Lee Friedlander.

This was heady attention for a photographer still in his twenties, but after a taste of art-world celebrity, Krause became wary of success. While he neither seeks nor shuns opportunities to publish or exhibit his work, he begrudges the energy required by self-promotion and distrusts the psychological drain. "You can get so caught up in what's happening," he says, "to the point you're always looking over your shoulder. Who's doing this, and how can you be part of that. With a certain amount of isolation, I can achieve the wonderful balance I need to create." He then adds, "Something funny about me doesn't really care about my career, but don't get me wrong, I would love to be recognized."

As a result of conflicting motivations, his photographs are at once widely published and relatively unknown. His work appears in seventy different books and catalogs, yet is surprisingly absent from many major museum collections. He has no gallery representation outside Houston and hasn't published a monograph larger than a booklet since 1972. Nevertheless, esteemed foundations and his peers have awarded him almost every major grant available to an American artist— some of them twice—and he receives frequent invitations to lecture and teach workshops in North and South America and in Europe.

An additional factor in Krause's elective obscurity is that his work does not follow any recognizable trend in contemporary art; neither critics nor the public can easily place his work in the pantheon. While Krause is cognizant of contemporary "isms," reads contemporary arts magazines, and attends many exhibitions, his pulse is as likely to change because of something he reads in a novel as by what he sees in a show. He haunts the historical wings of museums as well as contemporary installations. His sources include ancient Greece, the Italian Renaissance, Spanish Baroque, and subsequent periods. Simultaneously influenced by art and popular culture, he creates photographs that only incidentally overlap others' styles and seem to ignore "hot" new issues. His images are at once current and not of this or any specific time. "I really think I'm doing something very contemporary." says Krause. "Although not in the mainstream, I think I may be part of a broad undercurrent. And I wish to avoid what's commercial and faddish." As to how this affects his career, Krause says, "You can't worry about your images always being in front of the public or about what your images mean to them."[26]

Despite his reservations about the effects of public acclaim, Krause felt encouraged by his early recognition. In 1963 he became the first photographer to receive a Fulbright-Hays fellowship, allowing him to move to Spain with his family for nine months. He applied for a Fulbright because "I was desperate to change my life. I was just barely making a living, but wanted more time to do my own work." He chose Spain because most applicants requested other countries—creating less competition for Spanish fellowships—and because "I love Velásquez." This was the first time since his army stint that Krause was able to concentrate on photography without worrying about finances.

Compared with Philadelphia's Italian neighborhoods, Spain seemed simultaneously affable, familiar, and exotic. Though alien enough to be stimulating, it also resonated with enough that he knew for him to assimilate and photograph his impressions. The encounter prompted abundant new photographs that remain in Krause's portfolio after almost three decades. Especially memorable images made during the Fulbright fellowship include *Mocking*, *Shadow*, *La Linea*, *Dierick Bouts*, *Rocio*, and *John the Baptist* (pages 26, 29, 34, 36, 38, and 51).[27] Spain continues to be a fruitful place for him to work, and he returns whenever time and funds allow.

As previously discussed, life experiences, diverse arts, and Krause's own work concurrently incite him. For instance, *Shadow* (page 29) emanates from all three sources. Krause saw an elderly Spanish woman stalked by her own shadow. Rather than mirror the woman, her black trace on the stucco wall seemed to allude to a witch's large-nosed profile. At the same moment, the image also reminded him of a figure study that his wife had requested four years earlier when she was trying to lose weight. In the photograph, Pat's shadow appeared as a grotesque creature looming on the wall behind her. Krause perceived the distorted shadow as a projection of his wife's own image of low self-worth.

Beyond the graphic imitation of their source, shadows have been regarded as intimate revelations of the person. Some ancient civilizations and traditional societies have believed that the size and substance of one's shadow foretell one's fate. Some tribes believe that a person can be weakened or even killed if their shadow is "injured"; conversely, certain shadows, generally women's, can be dangerous to anyone who falls beneath them.[28] Krause instinctively acknowledged these beliefs when he photographed the old woman. To him, her dark trailing vestige connoted evil as we have learned to recognize it in folk tales, but the evil is directed at her, not us. The humped ancient's shadow mocks her, a visible echo shouted from her past and bearing witness to her character (or as many traditions would have it, to the character of old women). This and other Spanish photographs fully satisfy Krause's goal to "explore the idea of fantasy." As Mark Power realized, "His work is like the obverse side of Cartier-Bresson's coin: the strongest pictures seem to capture those indecisive moments when the spirit transcends the flesh; tenuous moments when stone turns to flesh, or flesh to stone, and myth and legend walk among us."[29]

In 1964 Krause traveled to Mexico on a commercial assignment for *Sports Illustrated*. To his street and *Qui Riposa* series, he now added photographs of religious statuary in a series later titled *Saints and Martyrs*. Catholic sculpture of saints and martyrs had fascinated him since childhood when his friends' mothers periodically insisted he attend church to save his non-Catholic soul from damnation. Then conducted in Latin, Catholic services were confusing to an untutored child. Krause was intimidated and captivated by the elaborate rituals and settings.

In the sixties, when he drove to Mexico on assignment, he visited churches because they constituted a major part of the culture. Since he didn't consciously focus on religious statuary, he was surprised upon returning from the trip to see that it dominated his contact sheets. Although he had previously photographed a Catholic martyr in Philadelphia's Little Italy (page 11) and saints in Spanish churches—including the seminal *John the Baptist*—he didn't sufficiently recognize the potential for a series on saints and martyrs until he saw the Mexican figures. Trusting his muse's lead, he has resolutely pursued the subject in churches throughout Central, South, and North America as well as Europe, even though Mexico remains his most fertile source.

The *Saints and Martyrs* photographs are "charged" with a multiplicity of meanings: what the statues mean to their locality, what they mean to Krause, and how people of different cultures and religions perceive them. They provoke a myriad of responses not only from the general public but from those grounded in Catholic theology and practices, and even from members of different orders within the Catholic church. In private discussions with Krause, members of the Jesuit order, for instance, have expressed strong disapproval of the statues themselves as well as of his photographic interpretations.

Statues of extreme, realistically portrayed violence and passion are found predominantly in Mexico—rarely in American Catholic churches. Some American viewers consequently assume

that the attitudes of the figures are of Krause's making, rather than of his discovery. They call the photographs blasphemous. "George Krause's works proved offensive to me and all that I stand for," wrote Missy Peaker to the school newspaper in Bakersfield, California. "In discussing the works with friends, their responses were consistent in that they were appalled by the shameful portrayals of Christ. In my mind, heart, and life, Christ stands as the victor, the opposite of how he was represented in the exhibit."[30]

In *Saints and Martyrs* visceral images of spirituality, sensuality, and violence intermingle to electrify the photographs. One might think that Krause's pictures were rooted in Paul Strand's powerful images of Mexican icons in *The Mexican Portfolio*. But as A. D. Coleman recognized, "The difference in intent is vast. Strand used the Mexican stations of the cross for basically polemical purposes: as emblems of an oppressive religion and, simultaneously, as metaphors for the sufferings of its believers. In Krause's images their religious nature is less significant than their embodiment of personal, private agonies."[31] Houston critic Mimi Crossley concurred. "Though the often grotesque expressionism of Mexican religious art is familiar to us through the photographs of Paul Strand," she wrote, "Krause's work is not removed and symbolic like Strand's. Krause's suffering saints with blood-dripped palms and flagellated bodies do not symbolize the agony of martyred death as a ritualistic way for us to understand it—they *are* death and suffering itself. The photographs are not about religion, but magic, fear and transference."[32]

In his book *The Cult of the Saints*, historian Peter Brown explores the role of tombs, shrines, relics, and pilgrimages relative to the sacred bodies of the saints.[33] Writing about religious practices between the third and sixth centuries, he shows how people living under harsh and sometimes barbaric conditions relied upon the merciful intercession of the holy dead to obtain justice and to help them accept their fates. Brown's eloquent account of those who gathered around saints' shrines in late antiquity presents antecedents for contemporary reverence paid to religious monuments. To and through these statues, worshippers express their fears and needs. People speak to the statues, read letters, even scream and weep.

In his book, Brown focuses on "the need for intimacy with a protector with whom [unlike gods or angels] one could identify as a fellow human being."[34] He describes the long drawn-out death of the martyr as "vibrant with the miraculous suppression of suffering. Memories of it set up an imaginative vortex in the minds of those who thronged to the shrine. This was all the more powerful because much of the overt expression of these sufferings had been blocked. The explicit image of the martyr was of a person who enjoyed the repose of Paradise and whose body was even now touched by the final rest of the resurrection. Yet behind the now-tranquil face of the martyr there lay potent memories of a process by which a body shattered by drawn-out pain had once been enabled by God's power to retain its integrity."[35]

Krause photographs statues depicting both saints at peace and those in the midst of their trial, and favors those whose suffering is most explicit. Although he has photographed serene saints in elegant settings, he has an aversion to anything that appears simply pretty or beautiful. "For me," he says, "beauty comes from a stone that's eroding, an image that's fading, a Christ that's in agony."[36] He believes these images stir less easily reached emotions in the viewer, which is a greater challenge than satisfying vague calls for Beauty.

Over the decades he has noted correlations between the quality of a country's economy and the types of religious statues presented. Poorer countries, such as Colombia, are more likely to choose Christ mocked by the soldiers, bloodied by a crown of thorns, and humiliated with a rope around his neck. The rope alludes to Christ having been bound to a pillar to be scourged. This station of the cross is known as *Ecce Homo* (Behold the Man) because, after the mocking of Christ, Pilate had the Saviour brought before the people. Telling them that he found no fault in Jesus, Pilate said, "Ecce Homo."[37] While poorer communities worship Christ in agony at the hands of other men, wealthier churches prefer Christ ascendent, and the Immaculate Madonna resplendent. As communities prosper, Krause has discovered that the bloodiest statues often disappear from the churches he repeatedly visits.

Selecting the most mutilated figures, Krause highlights their suffering even further by extracting the figures from their context. Just as context transforms the meaning of snapshots in *Qui Riposa*, isolating religious statues from their community of saints in the Houses of the Lord shifts the thrust of their impact from spiritual to physical and emotional states. It accentuates human suffering over the greater glory for which they suffered and the Church's promise of their transcendence. Krause seeks to transmit the psychological effect the statues have on those who empower them. By tightly framing each figure, he directs the viewer into a one-on-one encounter. More direct and less avoidable than one might prefer, the experience simulates the disconcerting affront of a speaker who gets too close in conversation, entering our personal space. The terms of the relationship intensify; that the statues reveal emotional and physical wounds heightens the already disturbing effect of their proximity.

Much as *Qui Riposa* features the work of journeyman photographers, *Saints and Martyrs* pays homage to the anonymous artisans who fashioned the statues. Krause is moved by the people who created these bloodied objects for comfort. He connects with their wellspring of passion. "These sculptures transcend most folk art," he says. "They are not conceptually motivated. The sculptor *felt* the suffering, and it allowed him to create something beyond himself and beyond the repetitive forms usually handed down among folk artists. I am responding to the artisan's passion and his unique vision."

The sculptors' personal identification with the saints and martyrs yielded statues that are "like us." Many of the figures were carved from wood, and then their hands and faces covered with polychrome gesso. Hair and clothing are often real and elaborate. The realistic aspects remind us that each saint was once living flesh. And as Peter Brown notes, saints are from a more contemporary time than Christ and frequently from the same locale as the church. Often the statues are about the size of an average parishioner. Mexico, where Indian and Spanish bloods and cultures blend and collide, produces saints with Spanish names and Aztec features (page 64). When photographing, Krause accentuates the life-like appearance of the figures, which further heightens the effect of the often graphically depicted wounds. Publisher Carole Kismaric recognized the disturbing result. In her introduction to Krause's portfolio from the series, she wrote, "The realistically sculpted figures, which we know to be symbols crafted of wood and plaster, are felt in the pictures to be intimately mortal—so relentlessly human, in fact, that they are almost unbearable."[38]

In each series, but especially in *Saints and Martyrs*, Krause dwells on the myriad personal qualities associated with long hair. In the photographs on pages iii, 33, 58, 62, 64, 66, 68, 71, 72, 74, 79, and 108, the central figure's hair is a major component of the picture's expressiveness. In the early example *Elephant Girl* (Philadelphia, 1965, page 33), a young woman watches a row of elephants. Her shimmering golden hair flows loosely, sharply contrasting with the muscular, coarsely wrinkled elephants' trunks. Her hair reflects light, youth, and femininity; the massive beasts are dark, primordial, and formidable.

In the religious statues Krause senses, and delights in, the ambivalence that exists in Christianity regarding long flowing hair, a symbol of both penitence and sexuality. Images of penitence derive from the episode related in Luke 7:37–38: "And, behold a woman in the city, which was a sinner,…stood at his [Jesus] feet behind him weeping, and began to wash his feet with tears, and did wipe them with the hairs of her head." According to scholar George Ferguson, "This Biblical story led to the custom of the hermits, and all those doing penance, of letting their hair grow long."[39] Similarly, a hair shirt evolved for penitence and mortification. This tradition contradicts such practices as covering women's hair in church and shaving nuns' heads, customs that have arisen because long flowing hair also connotes vanity and sexuality. St. Paul argued this position when he declared, "Is it comely that a woman pray unto God uncovered?"[40]

The Fulbright fellowship to Spain firmly set a pattern whereby Krause periodically packed up his family and traveled. In 1967 he won the first of two John Simon Guggenheim Memorial fellowships. He applied because, "I heard somewhere that nobody got a Guggenheim before they were thirty, and that year I was thirty." He also realized that he could most fruitfully pursue all three of his then-ongoing photography series in the churches, cemeteries, and streets of Europe. Traveling in a Volkswagen camper, George, Pat, George, Jr., and their baby, Katy, visited cities along the Mediterranean rim, from Turkey to Portugal.

The trip proved to be as productive as Krause's first European sojourn, but what remains constitutes half of what might have been. Five months into the trip, someone broke into the car and stole everything. Krause remembers, "Once or twice a week we'd stay in hotels to process film and shower. Every now and then I would take the film to a local photographer's lab and have them make contact sheets for me, so I could edit as I went along. I threw away the rejects and had a shoe box full of the kept negatives. We got into Barcelona late, and parked in front of the hotel. The thieves took clothes, the typewriter, Pat's cosmetics, cameras, and the shoe box. God, it was so stupid." Krause wept when he discovered the loss, and today speaks of the missing negatives wistfully. In the few months left on the fellowship, he unsuccessfully tried to recoup specific pictures by returning to their locations, but "that never works," he says. The end of the Guggenheim trip was in England and Ireland, neither of which evoked notable photographs for Krause. "I don't find I can work there," he acknowledges, "as well as I can in the Mediterranean countries."

In the interval between 1968 and 1975 Krause received his first National Endowment for the Arts grant, but primarily he worked as a commercial photographer. "When I came back from Europe in 1968," he recalls, "I decided I'd been poor long enough. I went from living on two thousand dollars annually to living on sixty thousand." His commercial clients ranged from pharmaceutical companies and advertising agencies to book publishers, including Time-Life Books, Penguin, and Houghton Mifflin, and magazines such as *Show*, *New York Times Sunday Magazine*, *Harper's Bazaar*, *McCall's*, *Sports Illustrated*, *Holiday*, and *Horizon*. "The hardest thing was to switch mentally from commercial to personal work, back and forth," Krause says today. "The phone rang all the time. I had a hard time saying no, so the only way I could do my own work was to take a month and go somewhere. It always took me two weeks to adjust. I'd finally be seeing with my own eyes and have only another week or two of the trip left. Then I'd be back, and the advertising benefited from the time off. I knew this wasn't working, but I tried to escape twice a year."

After several years at this pace, he decided that the quality of his life was getting worse, not better. "My kids didn't love me as much, and I was killing myself," he remembers. So, ironically, he returned to teaching, the profession he had declared he would never resume. In 1970 he founded the photography department at the Fleisher Art Memorial, where he had studied and modeled for portrait classes as a child. Later he accepted a number of teaching assignments, including a stint in 1972 at Brooklyn College while Walter Rosenblum took a sabbatical. Then, between 1973 and 1975, Krause succeeded Emmet Gowin as head of the photography department at Bucks County Community College.

In terms of his own work, teaching at Brooklyn was primarily important for something that occurred in the first week of classes. "To wake them up" on a hot September day, Krause facetiously suggested that the students do nude self-portraits. To his amazement, a few sensitive students became quite engaged in the assignment, so Krause decided to retain it in future courses as well as to hire models for nude studies in class. He, too, began to photograph the models, inaugurating his fourth series, *I Nudi*.

While teaching, Krause was still doing commercial work at a relentless pace. He kept working through an undiagnosed attack of appendicitis and almost died. His doctor insisted he change his lifestyle. So, when an old friend, George Bunker, moved from his position as dean at Philadelphia College of Art to chair the art department at the University of Houston and invited him to create a photography program, he accepted. Bunker revitalized the

department with considerable skill and energy. He added to the faculty painters Derek Boshier, Gael Stack, and John Alexander, sculptor James Surls, and photographers/video artists, Ed Hill and Suzanne Bloom.

Although Geoff Winningham taught photography at Rice University, few Houston institutions actively supported photography as fine art before 1975. It wasn't long, however, before Tony and Robin Cronin founded the Cronin Gallery for photography, and the Museum of Fine Arts, Houston began to collect photographs in a more extensive and systematic way. Krause was one of the first photographers in the Cronins' stable, and they gave him an exhibition in the gallery's first year. His work was also among the first photography to be acquired by the museum's new photography curator. A piece from *Qui Riposa* was exhibited in the museum's inaugural exhibition of new acquisitions in February 1977, and selections from *Saints and Martyrs* and *I Nudi* were exhibited in a small, one-person show in 1979.

Houston has proved to be a fruitful place for Krause to live and work. By age eighteen, he and his mother had lived in twenty-three different apartments. Now he has lived in Houston for fifteen years, since 1977 at the same address. His marriage, however, did not survive the move to Houston. In the late seventies, the couple divorced, and Pat moved to New Orleans.

In 1976, a year after accepting the job in Houston, Krause won his second Guggenheim fellowship and became the first photographer to win a Prix de Rome fellowship, allowing him to live and work for a year in Rome. Fellows at the American Academy are encouraged to eat one meal daily with other fellows. Krause enjoyed the interaction with people from many different disciplines. He tested his ideas against their wit and knowledge, and welcomed their conversations as useful stimuli for new photographs. While in Rome, he added images to his four bodies of work: *The Street, Qui Riposa, Saints and Martyrs,* and *I Nudi,* but he concentrated on his series of nudes. A few fellows posed for him. Others critiqued his portfolio. Two years later, he returned to the American Academy as photographer in residence; working in Rome was again a stimulating and productive experience.

Dividing one's attention among four ongoing series is atypical of artists. Most visual artists envision a theme that they formalize into an integrated series of artworks, pursuing the underlying idea until they have exhausted its variations. Such concentrated focus may last months or decades, depending on the richness of the initial idea and the artist's capacity and inclination to sustain the investigation, but eventually they move on to another formulation. Krause prefers to evolve his photographic and humanistic concerns in these four separate, yet interrelated, series. He admits, however, that he wouldn't mind adding another "child" to the other four, the youngest of which is now twenty years old.

The basic themes—sensuality, spirituality, mortality, and mystery—are not exclusive to any one series. Investigations often flow between them. Issues of spirituality and sensuality frequently merge in his work—for example, long hair on religious statues and saintly looking nude models in symbolic poses. *Saints and Martyrs* confronts both spiritual transcendence and mortal suffering. He also highlights the psychological effects of photographs found variously on a photographer's stand in *The Street*, tombstones in *Qui Riposa*, martyrs' garments in *Saints and Martyrs*, and the editing wall in *I Nudi*.

Formal devices also recur throughout his series. Artificial lights are encased with the saints, mounted on tombstones, and wrapped about nude models. In each instance, the lights date the picture in modern times and are a self-conscious acknowledgment of theatrical intent by whoever commissioned them. Further, Krause is fascinated with the possible evocations of flowing fabric and with the layered imagery in reflections, which he repeatedly explores in both *Saints and Martyrs* and *I Nudi*.

Unlike the other three series, the photographs in *I Nudi* are staged and, consequently, depend on Krause's ability to preconceive a scene. Once he imagines a potentially fruitful situation, he assembles the necessary ingredients and relies on commercial studio skills as well as on unanticipated interactions between the mustered artifacts and people.

Two uncommon values in Krause's nude studies are humor and his frequent use of figures that veer from the classical ideal. Besides his own middle-aged torso, he has photographed an anorectic, a grandmother, and a sagging shaman. But much of the series employs comely female models. Krause readily admits to being inspired by attractive women. And like other male artists, he has been accused of sleeping with his models. "My photographs," he responds, "[may] suggest...that I [am] getting more gratification out of photographing these nudes than just the making of images."[41] "Actually," he elaborates, "I find it all but impossible to mix lovemaking with the act of photographing. Nevertheless, a certain amount of [sexual tension] is inherent, and for me, necessary, when photographing." His desire to make a transcendent image is "helped greatly by encouraging in myself a fictional passion for the subject. In turn, the model can respond with a desire to fulfill the artist's goal of transcendence or with a narcissistic love for the attention being paid her, making love more to the camera than the photographer. At the first photographic session I'm anxious about both my fictional passion and my obligation to the model to create something special. In time, I realize I can control the situation and the amount of desire needed to create the image I'm after." Thus, actual seduction becomes less relevant than the viewer's vivid perception of Krause's fantasies about his shapely models. Often embodying the erotic tensions preceding sexual acts, the most successful photographs stir the viewer's imagination.

The traditional battle of the sexes is a major theme in *I Nudi*. By the term, Krause means both specific struggles between men and women as well as broader interpersonal battle lines drawn by society. He originally set forth the contest between a man and a woman, quite literally, in his street series with *Judo* (Puerto Rico, 1968, page 40). In the more general realm of psychological domination, Krause is aware of the intrinsic vulnerability of an undressed model in the presence of a dressed photographer and has dealt with the issue in various photographs—most universally when he photographed a naked man crouched on an examining table before an authority figure in a white coat. While most of us haven't posed for an artist, we know the anxiety of stripping for a doctor.

In another instance, Krause photographed himself clothed, standing by his studio desk while a nude model displayed herself on a chair. The model was his current com-

panion, a primary muse in the grand tradition of an artist working creatively with a particular model. Some of his most compelling photographs are of Victoria Long, including *Black Veil*, *Medusa*, *Swish*, and *Drawing* (pages 77, 79, 83, and 101). One critic, swooning over *Swish*, described Long as a heavenly being. "A floating canopy of cloth unfurls over the model's head," he wrote. "Half-seated, with one foot touching the ground, the woman looks as if she has just floated to earth."[42]

The only model who appears more frequently than Long in the *I Nudi* series is Krause himself. Photographs of him, and other male models, explore the nude less for its erotic potential than as a way to refer to favorite myths, art objects, and even religious symbols. For instance, in *Zurbarán Monk* (Rome, 1977, page 78), Krause demonstrates his admiration for paintings by the Spaniard Zurbarán, whose renderings of white-robed Franciscan priests he studied in museums and cathedrals throughout Spain. Despite his esteem for Zurbarán's skill, Krause is spoofing the paintings. And his decision to expose himself by lifting the robe is a modern gesture, reversing the anonymous hands that decked thousands of masterworks with fig leaves and loincloths throughout the nineteenth century. The challenge of lifting fig leaves, thus exposing himself psychologically as well as physically, continues to motivate him.[43]

Some of Krause's finest self-portraits are based on Greek

mythology. In *Bank of Lights* (Rome, 1976, page 87), Krause might be a modern-day Atlas, condemned by Zeus to support Heaven on his shoulders for eternity. Or is this Sisyphus in Hades, forever unable to reach the summit of the mount with his burden? What do the lights symbolize? Perhaps, like Atlas and Sisyphus, the artist angered the gods and they are inhibiting his progress? Critic Caroline Meline saw another parallel: as if Krause and his burden of lights "were Christ under the cross. He makes fun of himself. The artist is mocked as Christ was mocked; he is a sort of clown, which is the image Picasso used to depict himself, as did the painter Rouault. Only Krause has left off the clown suit and wears only the emperor's new clothes."[44]

Krause titled another photograph of Victoria Long and himself *Medusa* (Rome, 1980, page 79) because she, lying in the tub with her hair flying out from her head, reminded him of the winged monster with glaring eyes and serpent locks. According to the myth (which, among other issues, represents the classic battle of the sexes), Medusa's visage was so ugly that all who gazed at it were petrified with fright. Armed by Athena with a brightly polished shield, Perseus used the shield to deflect Medusa's deadly gaze and deployed her reflected image to behead her. That Perseus was advised by Athena, patroness of artisans, seems particularly apt here. If Victoria is Medusa, then George, with his bare leg entering the picture, is Perseus, and his camera is his shield. Many photographers acknowledge that their cameras let them view sights that might otherwise paralyze them. One young woman could photograph in the morgue only if she entered the door with her camera to her eye. Margaret Bourke-White said that her camera made her feel invulnerable. While on the battlefield, she had to remind herself repeatedly that her camera, at best, protected only her face, leaving the rest of her body exposed.

In *Editing Wall* (Rome, 1979, page 91), a naked Krause appears frantic as he searches a wall of his photographs. The number of images, some of them spilling onto the floor, and

Krause's striving reach suggest that a monumental task has been undertaken. The wall becomes a giant war board on which he maps the strategy of expressing himself. His nakedness is a common-enough reference to artists' vulnerability when their work is on display.

By far the most controversial of Krause's self-portraits is *Question Mark* (Houston, 1983, page 93) in which he wears a mask with a long nose and studies his own erection. The whimsical quality of a child playing "I see you" is offset by his straining body, down to the curling toes. In erotic imagery, crispation of toes frequently signifies orgasm, but here the gesture may be Krause using part of his body to fool or entice another part into action.

The humor, the sexual and muscular tensions, and the exposure of erect genitalia have stirred opposing but equally passionate responses to the picture. Krause intended it to be "vulnerable and humorous," but posed for it himself because he was too embarrassed to ask someone else. Men are generally more offended by the picture than women, many of whom find it amusing. When one man dismissed the photograph because its only message was that men care too much for their penises, Krause responded, "Don't they?"

Looking at Krause's erection might make men uncomfortable because it opens men's sexuality and their pubic region to public scrutiny, comparison, and discussion in unfamiliar ways. Women's bodies have been the subject of art, advertising, and entertainment for centuries. Women, for better or worse, have grown up evaluating their sexual endowments and having their bodies compared with published photographs of other women. Most men have experienced such comparison only in locker rooms and in the military, in the exclusive company of other men.

Both men and women are often embarrassed when they unexpectedly confront nudes, particularly if genitalia are exposed. In viewing photographs, we stand where the camera stood. The photographer has gone, and we are left in a public space with the subject. A viewer may compare the experience to peeking through a keyhole—and dread being caught looking. This feeling becomes exaggerated when there is eye contact between the model and the camera—therefore between the model and the viewer.

Krause is not immune to his audience's discomfort. He admits that photographing nudes is to some degree inherently the act of an invader. "Even in a comfortable environment," he wrote, "the camera's presence (and then our own) intrudes upon the nude, and when an awareness of technique (special lighting and camera effects) is added, along with...[a] concern for props and costume, the intrusion must be that much greater."[45]

After watching viewers' embarrassed reactions and sudden retreats from his small-scale prints of nudes (most images are printed 5 x 7 inches), Krause decided to enlarge the images onto 16 x 20–inch sheets of paper. A small print can be viewed by only one person at one time, and increases the viewer's sense of forced intimacy. Krause has observed that audiences are more comfortable and candid about their reactions to the nudes when he enlarges the images.

Transformation is another theme that fascinates Krause. Whether it is Zeus metamorphosing himself to seduce a mortal or the biological conversion of a caterpillar into a butterfly, Krause relishes the drama embodied in changing appearances as well as using physical transformation as a metaphor for emotional or spiritual change. In two of his photographs, *Dog Girl* (Austin, 1981, page 80) and *Turtle Man* (Austin. 1981, page 95), we perceive by analysis that both a person and an animal are present before the camera, but little else is certain. The people have no identity or specific age. The occasion or cause of the apparent union is open to speculation. Are we to induce shared physical or behavioral attributes—the ferociousness of the snapping turtle and the warrior's legs of the man? Or should we concentrate on differences—the delicate softness of a girl's body versus the jowly, slobbering beast?

Most of Krause's images are too evocative to accept on literal terms alone. It is implausible that *Turtle Man* occurred because this man wanted to demonstrate his physical prowess, and a giant snapping turtle was the handiest massive weight to lift. Is it, instead, allegorical? By having a man lift a turtle is Krause inverting the myth of a cosmic turtle supporting the world? Or is he relying on a turtle's primeval associations? Is this a mythic combat between a hero and an animal-monster that must be slain before order can be reestablished?

Some viewers have been disturbed by the sexual evocations in the picture. One woman even read the animal's tail as a phallus and expressed alarm at the picture's explicitness. Such narrow sensibilities dismay Krause. He delights in layers of interpretation and even conflicting readings. For example, a dog-headed body could signify a lascivious girl or a faithful one.

Krause explores intensely personal themes rooted in basic human concerns: sensuality, spirituality, mortality, and mystery. When I designated these as "universal issues," he objected. Such sweeping claims for his work seem presumptuous to him. Nevertheless, these concerns consistently and naturally occur in life and variously impact every generation. What may be uncommon is Krause's willingness to publicly confront his fears, percep-

tions, and experiences about these vital components of existence. He transgresses the norms of polite society, exposing what many people prefer to leave unseen.

His work is perpetually relevant because his issues are basic and vital to the human condition. Few viewers leave his exhibitions unmoved—be it by indignation, horror, pathos, or wonder. If Krause succeeds on his own terms, their minds and imaginations as well as their feelings will have been affected.

Notes

1   Telephone conversation between an anonymous museum member and the author, February 1978. Later that year the publisher of the University of Houston yearbook refused to print twenty pages featuring Krause's photographs of his students posing and photographing male and female nude models. When the university's chancellor upheld the publisher's decision, the yearbook staff, backed by the student government, voted to leave those yearbook pages blank except for a brief statement by Krause in which he acknowledged that the nude has a history as a controversial subject in art and that "our times [in particular] seem to find it difficult to accept many serious photographs of nudes." He defended his classes as "an attempt to deal with the nude in a contemporary way executed with a modern medium (photography). But these photographs even though they

include nudity, really are about the students, the places and the times." Krause's portfolio at the end of the yearbook was designed to parallel another twenty-page portfolio introducing the book. The front matter was created by the other two photography faculty at the university, Ed Hill and Suzanne Bloom. Like Krause, but in their own style, they photographed the campus and its students. The student government published a booklet of Krause's censored photographs titled Houstonian '78 Supplement (Houston: University of Houston Student Publications, 1978). His statement was printed in both the supplement and the yearbook, Houstonian 1978, 484.

2   Lloyd Goodrich, Thomas Eakins, His Life and Work (New York: Whitney Museum, 1933). Quoted in Fairfield Porter, Thomas Eakins (New York: George

Braziller, 1959), 24.

3   J[ames] S. W[hitney], "Art?", Penn Monthly 8 (May 1877): 369–70. Quoted in David Sellin, The First Pose (New York: W.W. Norton & Company, 1976), 56–57.

4   Porter, 26.

5   Ibid., 27.

6   Unless otherwise cited, all quotes by Krause are from an interview with the author at Krause's home on 16 January 1991 or from subsequent telephone conversations.

7   Patricia Johnson, "The Artist," Houston Chronicle Zest Magazine, 5 August 1984.

8   Joline Gutierrez Krueger, "Arts: Krause Photographs Bits of Humanity," Daily Lobo (University of N. Mex.), 6 April 1987.

9   Paul Cava and M. E. Mankus, "Interview with George Krause," Philadelphia Arts Exchange, January 1977.

10 J. E. Cirlot, A Dictionary of Symbols, 2d ed. (New York: Philosophical Library, 1971), 26–28.

11 Mother Goose: Her Rhymes (Akron, Ohio: Saalfield Publishing Company, 1915), unpaginated.

12 Mark Power, introduction to George Krause 1 (Haverford, Penn.: Toll & Armstrong, 1972), unpaginated.

13 Nessa Forman, "Krause: Technical Eye, Sensitive Heart," Philadelphia Bulletin, 24 January 1982.

14 For further information on the Photo League see: Anne Tucker, "Photographic Crossroads: The Photo League," Journal (National Gallery of Canada), no. 25 (6 April 1978): 1–8. Distributed as a special supplement to Afterimage.

15 Krause remembers viewing prints at the Philadelphia Museum of Art with Carl Zigrosser, the legendary curator of prints and drawings. Until the museum began to collect photographs systematically in 1967, most of its photographs were gifts, including those by Krause. The most important of the museum's early acquisitions was a bequest of Alfred Stieglitz photographs from his estate. However, in 1962, Krause, Weiss, and Don Donaghy formed a short-lived gallery called the Photography Place, and the museum purchased a print of Ansel Adams' Moonrise over Hernandez for seventy-five dollars.

16 Murray Weiss, "Introduction: Two Young Philadelphians, Don Donaghy and George Krause," Contemporary Photographer, Fall 1962, unpaginated.

17 "Young Talent USA," Art in America, June 1963, 54. In subsequent statements Krause has changed the quote to read, "to explore the idea of fantasy with the real medium of photography."

18 Barbara G. Walker, The Woman's Dictionary of Symbols and Sacred Objects (San Francisco: Harper & Row, 1988), 378–79. Steven Olderr, Symbolism: A Comprehensive Dictionary (Jefferson, N. C.: McFarland & Company, 1986), 68–69.

19 Arno Minkkinen, "George Krause," in Contemporary Photographers, 2d ed. Edited by Colin Naylor (Chicago and London: St. James Press, 1988), 555.

20 Cava.

21 A.D. Coleman, "Latent Image: Death as a Living Reality," Village Voice, 13 July 1972.

22 Caroline Meline, "Photographer wins global plaudits, but his heart's in Phila," Philadelphia Inquirer, 15 January 1982.

23 Joseph Campbell, The Masks of God: Creative Mythology (New York: Viking Press, 1968), 503.

24 In late 1961 Krause showed Steichen the first prints in his Qui Riposa series, but none were purchased. Grace Mayer, Steichen's assistant, wrote, "Mr. Steichen commented (and I quote): 'Very nice! Very sensitive, fine feeling. I like his title.'" (Letter in possession of George Krause)

25 The book for "The Photographer's Eye" was published in 1966 while the exhibition was still touring.

26 Cava.

27 Ten of the sixty photographs published in Krause's first book were made on that trip.

28 Walker, 353. Sir James Frazer, The New Golden Bough, abridged. Edited with notes and foreword by Theodor H. Gaster (New York: New American Library, 1959), 201–203.

29 Mark Power, "George Krause: A Quiet Intensity," Lightwork, November 1974, 11.

30 Missy Peaker, "Artwork Unappreciated," Renegade Rip (Bakersfield College, Calif.), 20 February 1990.

31 Coleman.

32 Mimi Crossley, "Houston's first whole look at work of photographer who out-classicizes the cool ones," Houston Post, 19 February 1978.

33 Peter Brown, The Cult of the Saints: Its Rise and Function in Late Christianity (Chicago: University of Chicago Press, 1981).

34 Ibid., 61.

35   *Ibid., 80.*

36   *Maralyn Lois Polak, "Interview: George*
     Krause, 'My Business is to Search Out
     Images,' " Philadelphia Inquirer,
     6 June 1975.

37   *John 19:4–5, cited in Father Agustin*
     Moreno, An Age of Gold: Three
     Centuries of Paintings for Old Ecuador
     (Miami: Vizcaya Museum and Gardens,
     1983), 38.

38   *George Ferguson,* Signs and Symbols in
     Christian Art *(New York: Oxford*
     University Press, 1955), 22.

39   *Ibid., 26.*

40   *1 Cor. 11:13.*

41   *George Krause, "The Naked Truth,"*
     Image *(Houston Center for Photography)*
     2 (September 1983): 18.

42   *Jonathan G. Katz, "Around the Galleries:*
     Irreverent nudes from a native son,"
     Philadelphia Bulletin, *(day ?) April 1981.*

43   *Two books that have influenced Krause*
     are Leo Steinberg, The Sexuality of
     Christ in Renaissance Art and in Modern
     Oblivion *(New York: A Pantheon/October*
     Book, 1984), and Theodore Bowie
     and Cornelia V. Christenson, eds.,
     Studies in Erotic Art *(New York:*
     Basic Books, 1970).

44   *Meline.*

45   *Krause.*

The Street

23

24

DIERICK BOUTS

36

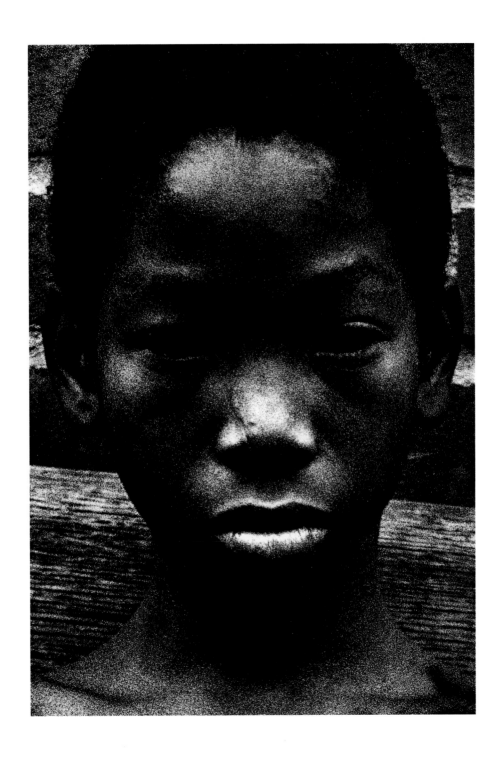

40

Saints and Martyrs

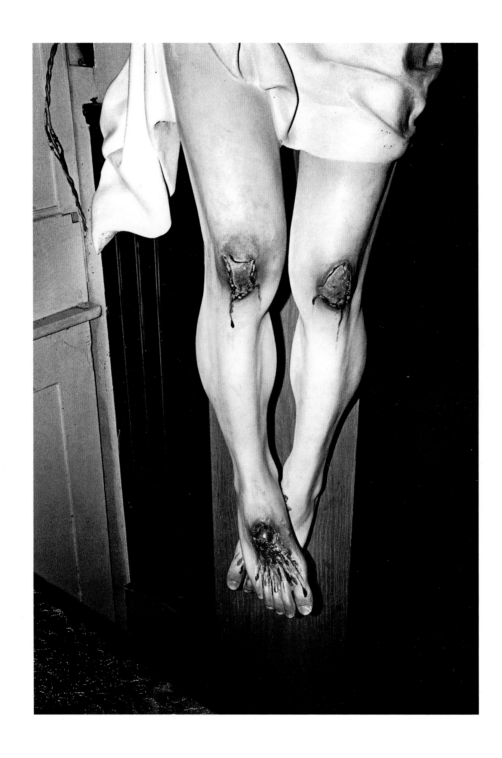

60

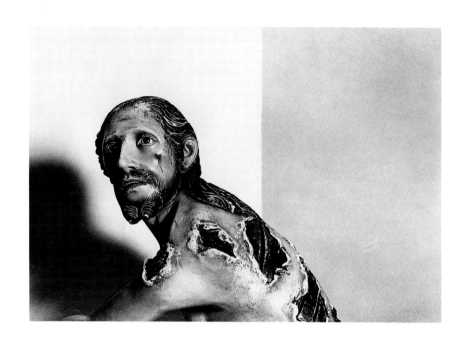

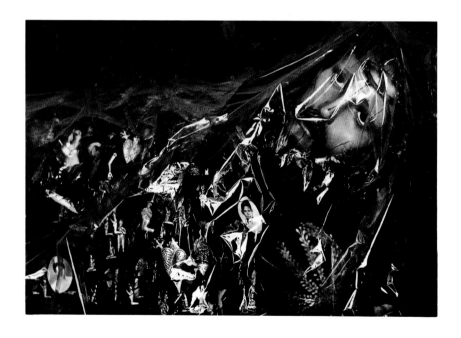

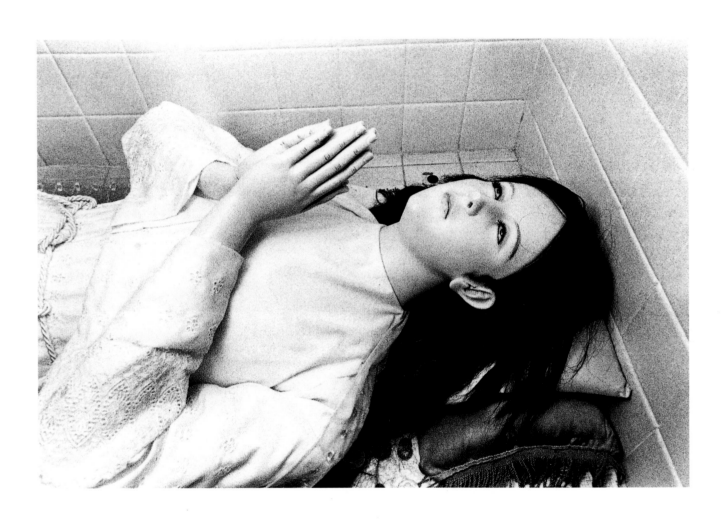

I *Nudi*

82

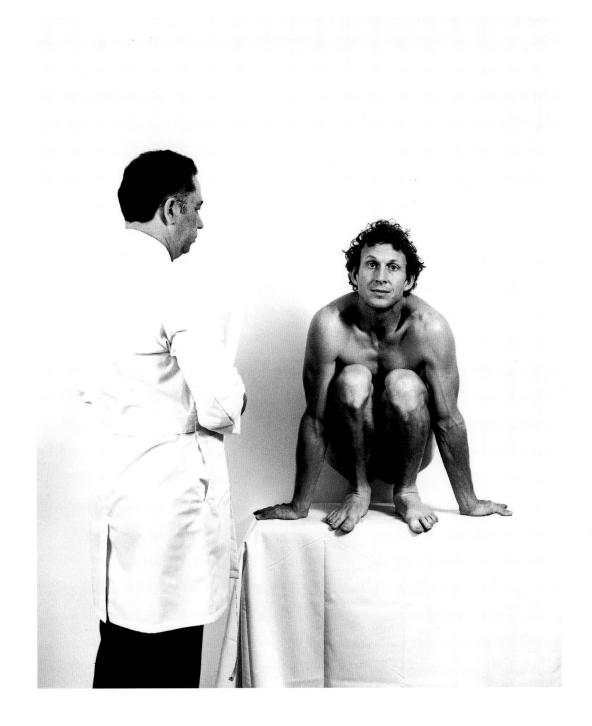

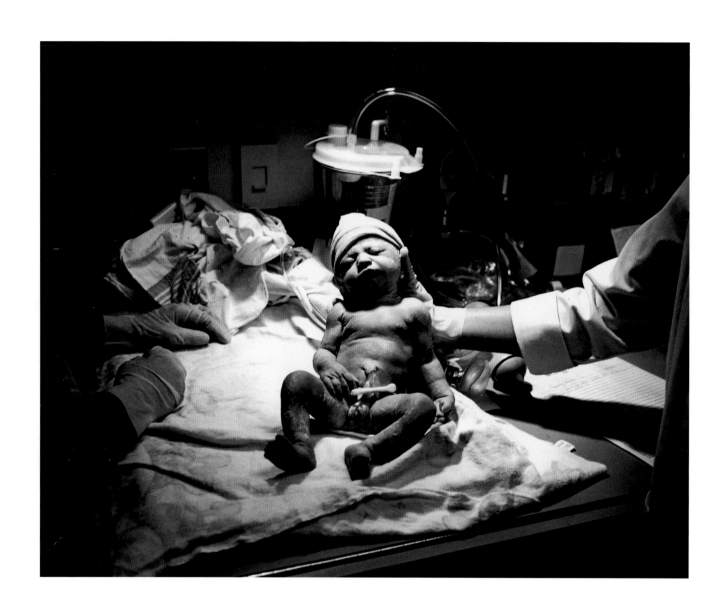

Qui Riposa

IN MEMORIA

DAVID ED ANGELO

DEPORTATI DAI NAZI-FASCISTI NEL 1943

George Krause
by Elizabeth Claud

Born Philadelphia, 24 January 1937

Attended Philadelphia College of Art
1954–57, 1959–60

Resides Houston

Professional Experience

1975–present
Professor of Art, University of Houston

Summer 1979
Director, "Venezia '79—La fotografia"
(Venice Photographic Biennial)

Summer 1978
Associate Professor, Instituto Allende,
San Miguel de Allende, Mexico

1973–75
Associate Professor, Head of Photography

Department, Bucks County Community
College, Newton, Pa.

1972–73
Instructor of Photography, Brooklyn
College, N.Y.

1970–72
Instructor of Photography, Samuel S.
Fleisher Art Memorial, Philadelphia

1957–59
U.S. military service

1956–57
Instructor (part-time), Samuel S. Fleisher
Art Memorial, Philadelphia

Instructor (part-time), painting and drawing,
Swarthmore College, Pa.

Grants and Awards

1986
Cultural Arts Council of Houston

1985
National Endowment for the Arts,
filmmaking

1983
Unicolor Grant

1979
Photographer in Residence, American
Academy in Rome

National Endowment for the Arts

1976
First Prix de Rome in photography

Guggenheim Fellowship

1975
Commission for Bicentennial, Philadelphia

1973
National Endowment for the Arts

1970
Philadelphia College of Art Alumni Award

1967
Guggenheim Fellowship

1966
Commission from Citizens' Council on City
Planning and the Philadelphia Foundation

1963
Fulbright-Hays Fellowship to Spain

Selected Individual Exhibitions

1990
Art Gallery, Bakersfield College, Calif.

Galería Spectrum, Zaragoza, Spain

Harris Gallery, Houston

New England Photographic Workshops,
New Milford, Conn.

1988
Harris Gallery, Houston

Maine Photographic Workshops,
Rockport, Maine

1987
Allen Street Gallery, Dallas

Film in the Cities, Minneapolis/St. Paul

Photographers Gallery, London

Torino Fotografia, Turin, Italy

1985
f.32 Foto Galerie, Amsterdam

Harris Gallery, Houston

Torino Fotografia, Turin, Italy

1984
McKillop Gallery, Salve Regina College,
Newport, R.I.

1983
Chrysler Museum, Norfolk, Va.

1982
Amarillo Art Museum, Tex.

Burton Gallery, Toronto

Milwaukee Center for Photography

Pennsylvania Academy of Fine Arts,
Philadelphia

1981
Focus Gallery, San Francisco
(with Joseph Jachna)

Mancini Gallery, Philadelphia

Mitzi Landau Gallery, Los Angeles

Morris Gallery, Philadelphia
(retrospective 1960–81)

1980
American Academy in Rome

Hills Gallery, Denver

1979
Milwaukee Center for Photography

Pennsylvania Academy of Fine Arts,
Philadelphia

Rochester Institute of Technology, N.Y.

1978
Agatha Gaillard Gallery, Paris

Museum of Fine Arts, Houston

Witkin Gallery, New York

1977
American Academy in Rome

Fotografia Gallery, Los Angeles

Gallery of Photography, Vancouver

1976
Afterimage Gallery, Dallas

Cronin Gallery, Houston

Enjay Gallery, Boston

Museo de Bellas Artes, Bogotá

Photopia Gallery, Philadelphia

1975
Milwaukee Center for Photography

Philadelphia Print Club
(with Norman Ackroyd, printmaker)

1974
Gallery of Photography, Vancouver

Museo de Bellas Artes, Caracas

Photopia Gallery, Philadelphia

1973
Briarcliff College, Briarcliff Manor, N.Y.

Fotografia Gallery, Los Angeles
(retrospective 1958–65)

Pennsylvania Academy of Fine Arts,
Philadelphia

1972
International Museum of Photography at the
George Eastman House, Rochester, N.Y.

Moravian College, Bethlehem, Pa.

Pennsylvania State University,
University Park

Witkin Gallery, New York
(with Philip Trager)

1971
Photographer's Place, Berwyn, Pa.

1970
Witkin Gallery, New York

1969
Museo de Bellas Artes, Caracas

1966
Citizens' Council on City Planning,
Philadelphia

Kenmore Galleries, Philadelphia

1964
Philadelphia Art Alliance

1963
Pennsylvania State University,
University Park

Selected Group Exhibitions

1990
"Me, Myself and I: A Photographic Self Portrait Exhibition," Allen Street Gallery,
Dallas

"Re: memory: Four Photographers Explore
Images of the Private Past," Birmingham
Museum of Art, Ala. (with Lorie Novak,
Larry Sultan, and Anne Turyn)

1989
"Light Years," Kuhn Gallery, University of
Maryland, Baltimore

"Photographers: Their Own Image," Texas
Photographic Society, Austin, Tex.

"Sections," International Center for
Photography, New York (touring exhibition)

1988
"Evocative Presence," Museum of Fine Arts,
Houston

"Nine Contemporary Photographers: The
Presence of the Sublime," San Antonio
Museum of Art

"The Nude: Male/Female," G. Ray Hawkins
Gallery, Los Angeles

"One + One," Glassell School of Art,
Museum of Fine Arts, Houston

"Three Houston Photographers," Harris
Gallery, Houston (with Peter Brown and
Geoff Winningham)

1987
"Ten Texas Photographers," Abilene
Fine Arts Museum, Tex.

"Thirty Works By Thirty Artists," Glassell
School of Art, Museum of Fine Arts,
Houston

1986
"Brown/Krause/Winningham," Harris
Gallery, Houston

"Swimming Pools," St. Canon Gallery,
Amsterdam

"Ten Texas Photographers," Abilene
Fine Arts Museum, Tex.

1985
"Posteriors," Benteler Gallery, Houston

"Suspended Animation," 1600 Cullen
Center, Houston

1984
"American Photography Today 1984,"
University of Denver

"The Directed Image," G.H. Dalsheimer
Gallery, Baltimore

"George Krause and John Gossage Photographs," University of Maryland, Baltimore

"1969–1984: A Selection from the Years,"
Witkin Gallery, New York

"Photographic Masterpieces from 60 International Galleries," AIPAD, New York

"Self Images," Fire House, Houston

"Three Houston Photographers," Harris
Gallery, Houston (with Peter Brown and
Geoff Winningham)

1982
"Art from Houston in Norway,"

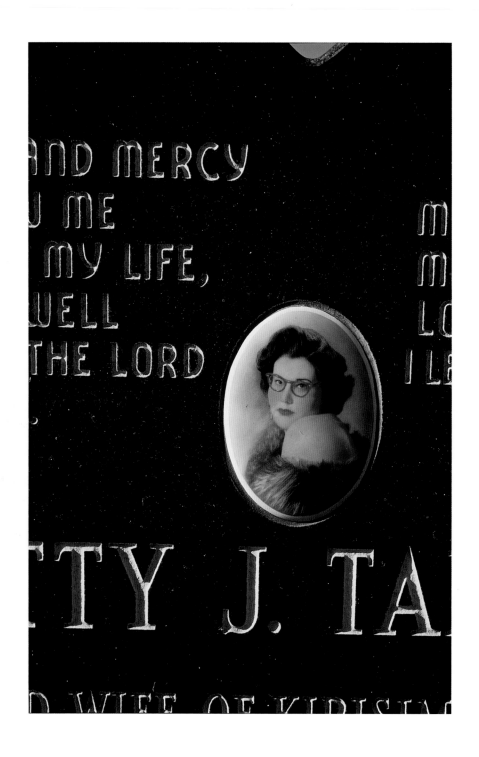

Stavenger, Norway

1981

"American Children," Museum of Modern Art, New York

"New American Nudes: Recent Trends and Attitudes," Creative Photography Gallery, MIT, Cambridge

"New Directions—The Nude," MIT, Cambridge

"Permanent Photography Collection," San Antonio Museum of Art

"Salute! Five Houston Artists," Houston Festival '81, Alley Theater, Houston

"Texas Photo Sampler," Washington Project for the Arts, Washington, D.C.

1980

"Annual Fellows Exhibition," American Academy in Rome

1979

"Self as Subject," Scudder Gallery, Durham, N.H.

"The Anthony G. Cronin Memorial Collection," Museum of Fine Arts, Houston

1978

"Mirrors and Windows: Photography Since 1960," Museum of Modern Art, New York (toured U.S. 1978–80)

1977

"Annual Fellows Exhibition," American Academy in Rome

"Brooklyn College Art Department," Robert Schoelkopf Gallery and Davis and Long

Gallery, New York

"Houston Photography Invitational," Galveston Arts Center, Tex.

"Target Collection of American Photography," Museum of Fine Arts, Houston (toured U.S.)

1976

"New Portfolios," Montgomery Art Gallery, Pomona College, Calif. (toured to Friends of Photography 1977)

"Philadelphia: Three Centuries of Art," Philadelphia Museum of Art

1974

"Photography in America," Whitney Museum of American Art, New York

1971

"Contemporary Photographs 1," Fogg Art Museum, Harvard University, Cambridge

"New Acquisitions," Philadelphia Museum of Art

1970

"Contemporary Photography," Pennsylvania Academy of Fine Arts, Philadelphia

"The Photography Collection Grows, Gifts and Purchases 1968–1969," Worcester Art Museum, Mass.

1969

"Award Winning Alumni," Philadelphia College of Art

"New Photography U.S.A.," Museum of Modern Art, New York (traveled to Europe and Latin America)

1967

"The Camera As Witness," Montreal

"Photography in the Twentieth Century," National Gallery of Canada, Ottawa (toured U.S. and Canada 1967–73)

"Steichen Photo Center Installation," Museum of Modern Art, New York

1966

"Art in Embassies," Bucharest, Romania, organized by the Museum of Modern Art, New York

"Photography: A Current Report," organized by the Museum of Modern Art, New York (traveling exhibition)

1965

"Recent Acquisitions," Museum of Modern Art, New York

"Photography in America," Whitney Museum of American Art, New York

1964

"The Photographer's Eye," Museum of Modern Art, New York

"Contemporary Photographers 1," International Museum of Photography at George Eastman House, Rochester, N.Y. (also known as "Six Photographers," toured U.S. until 1970; with Carl Chiarenza, Nicholas Dean, Bill Hanson, Don Donaghy, and Jack Stuler)

"Exposición de artistas becarios Fulbright 63–64 en España," Instituto de Estudiantes Norteamericanos, Madrid

Philadelphia Art Alliance

1963

"Five Unrelated Photographers," Museum of Modern Art, New York (with Ken Heyman, Jerome Liebling, Minor White, and Garry Winogrand)

"Photography 63/An International Exhibition," traveling exhibition sponsored by the International Museum of Photography at George Eastman House (originated at the N. Y. State Exposition, Syracuse, toured U.S. and Canada)

"Three Photographers: Carl Chiarenza, George Krause, Jack Stuler," George Eastman House, Rochester, N.Y.

1962

"Two Young Philadelphians," Photographer's Place, Kenmore Gallery, Philadelphia (with Don Donaghy)

1960

"Recent Acquisitions," Museum of Modern Art, New York

Monographs

Brown, Rosellen, and George Krause. *Qui Riposa: Alternative Lives*. New Haven, Conn., 1987.

Krause, George. *George Krause 1*. Introduction by Mark Power. Haverford, Pa.: Toll & Armstrong, 1972.

— . *I Nudi*. Philadelphia: Mancini Gallery, 1980.

Selected Portfolios

Krause, George. *George Krause 1960–1970*. Introduction by Mark Power. New York: Mancini Gallery, 1980.

— . *Saints and Martyrs*. Introduction by Carole Kismaric. Philadelphia: Photopia Gallery, 1975.

Films

Krause, George. *Mysteries*. 16 mm. 5 min., 20 sec. Work in progress. Krause began this animation of still photographs in the late 1960s. Most of the images were shot in Spain, although some were shot in Mexico and South America. *Mysteries* is an exploration of Holy Week activities in Spanish cultures with Spanish music soundtrack. The film appeared on "Territories" (a television series produced by the Southwest Alternate Media Project, Houston) in 1984.

— . *Untitled*. 16 mm, approx. 3 min. Work in progress. Krause satirizes the San Francisco Erotic Film Festival. The film was shown at the Harris Gallery, Houston, in 1985.

Selected Books

Brash, Edward, ed. *Photography Year 1979*. New York: Time-Life Books, 1979, 42.

Durniak, John, ed. *Photography Annual 1966*. New York: Ziff-Davis, 1966, 166–71.

— , ed. *Photography Annual 1968*. New York: Ziff-Davis, 1968, 112–13.

Editors of Time-Life Books. *The Art of Photography*. New York: Time-Life Books, 1971, 100–101, 224.

— . *Light and Film*. New York: Time-Life Books, 1970, 38.

Ferebee, Ann. *A History of Design From the Victorian Era to the Present: A Survey of the Modern Style in Architecture, Interior Design, Industrial Design and Photography*. New York: Van Nostrand Reinhold, 1970, 119.

Flattau, John, Ralph Gibson, and Arne Lewis, eds. *Contact: Theory*. New York: Lustrum Press, 1980, 92–95.

International Center for Photography. *Eighth Year Report*. New York: ICP, 1982, 38.

International Museum of Photography at George Eastman House. *American Photography in the 1960s*. Rochester, N.Y.: University of Rochester and International Museum of Photography at George Eastman House, 1990.

Kismaric, Carole, and Jay Brennan, eds. *The Great Themes*. New York: Time-Life Books, 1970, 21.

Kismaric, Susan. *American Children*. New York: Museum of Modern Art, 1980, 31–32.

Korn, Jerry, ed. "Krause's Favorites." In *Photography Year 1973*, 160–62. New York: Time-Life Books, 1973.

— , ed. "The Major Shows/Old Masters and New." In *Photography Year 1982*, 80, 87. New York: Time-Life Books, 1982.

Krause, George. *Houstonian '78 Supplement*. Houston: University of Houston Student Publications, 1978.

— . "Intensification." In *Darkroom*. Edited by Eleanor Lewis, 105–15. New York: Lustrum Press, 1977; reprint, "Darkroom: George Krause," *Camera: International Magazine for Photography* 57 (May 1978): 33–37.

Malanga, Gerard, ed. *Scopophilia: The Love of Looking*. New York: Alfred van der Mark, 1985, 50–53.

Maloney, Tom, ed. *U.S. Camera '62 Photography Annual*. New York: Duell, Sloane & Pearce, 1961, 142, 201.

—, ed. *U.S. Camera International Pictures 1963*. New York: Duell, Sloan, & Pearce, 1962, 174.

—, ed. *1967 U.S. Camera World Annual*. New York: U.S. Camera Publishing Company, 1966, 82–83.

Mason, Jerry, ed. *Family of Children*. New York: Grossett & Dunlap, 1977, 189.

Mason, Robert G., ed. *The Camera*. New York: Time-Life Books, 1970, 82–83.

—, ed. *The Print*. New York: Time-Life Books, 1970, 142–43.

Maye, Patricia, and Jay Brennan, eds. *Special Problems*. rev. ed. New York: Time-Life Books, 1981, 200–201.

Minkkinen, Arno. *New American Nudes: Recent Trends and Attitudes*. New York: Morgan & Morgan, 1981, 3–6.

—. "George Krause." In *Contemporary Photographers*. 2d ed. Edited by Colin Naylor, 553–55. Chicago and London: St. James Press, 1988.

Neil, Kaye, picture ed. *Photographing Children*. New York: Time-Life Books, 1971, 12, 18, 114, 194, 210–13.

Pennsylvania Academy of Fine Arts. *Searching Out the Best 1978/1988: A Tribute to the Morris Gallery of the Pennsylvania Academy of Fine Arts*. Philadelphia: Pennsylvania Academy of Fine Arts, 1988, 134–35.

Porter, John Paul, ed. *Photography Year 1973*. New York: Time-Life Books, 1973, 160–62.

Sandweiss, Martha, Roy Flukinger, and Anne W. Tucker, eds. *Contemporary Texas: The Photographic Portrait*. Austin: Texas Monthly Press, 1986, 157–70.

Shaw, Renata. *A Century of Photographs 1846–1946*. Washington, D.C.: Library of Congress, 77.

Szarkowski, John. *Looking at Photographs: 100 Pictures from the Collection of the Museum of Modern Art*. New York: Museum of Modern Art, 1973, 186–87.

Traub, Charles, and Luigi Balerini, eds. *Italy, Observed in Photography and Literature*. New York: Rizzoli International, 1988, 131.

Witkin, Lee D. *A Ten Year Salute: A Selection of Photographs in Celebration, The Witkin Gallery 1960–1969*. Danbury, N.H.: Addison House, 1969, 167.

Witkin, Lee D., and Barbara London. *The Photograph Collector's Guide*. Boston: New York Graphic Society, 1979, 175–76.

Catalogs

Abilene Fine Arts Museum. *Ten Texas Photographers*. Abilene, Tex.: Abilene Fine Arts Museum, 1986.

Agee, William, and Anne W. Tucker. *The Target Collection of American Photography*. Houston: Museum of Fine Arts, Houston, 1977, 60.

Arroyo, Miguel G. *Krause o lo insólito en lo cotidiano*. Caracas: Museo de Bellas Artes, 1974.

Art League of Houston. *Texas Visions: A Celebration of Texas Artists*. Houston: Art League of Houston, 1985, 42.

Brauer, David, ed. *Art From Houston in Norway 1982*. Stavenger, Norway, 1982, 31.

Città di Torino Assessorato per la Cultura. *Auto Scatto (Mostra fotografica su 30 anni di vita, società, sport, protagonista, l'auto)*. Turin, Italy: Editoriale Domus, 1986, 177.

Doty, Robert, ed., *Photography in America*. New York: Greenwich House, 1974, 224.

Edwards, Jim. *Contemporary Photographers: The Presence of the Sublime*. San Antonio: San Antonio Museum of Art, 1988, 12.

Fogg Art Museum. *Contemporary Photographs 1*. Cambridge: Fogg Art Museum, Harvard University, 1971.

Foresta, Merry Amanda. *Exposed and Developed: Photography Sponsored by the National Endowment for the Arts*. Washington, D.C.: Smithsonian Institution Press for the National Endowment for the Arts, 1984, 92–93.

Hadler, Mona, and Jerome Viola. *Past and Present 1942–77*. Brooklyn, N.Y.: Brooklyn College Art Department, 1977, 64.

Hitchcock, Barbara, ed. *Selections 4:*

The International Polaroid Collection.
Cambridge, Mass.: Polaroid Corporation,
1988, unpaginated.

Houston FotoFest. *FotoFest 88: The International Month of Photography.* Houston:
Houston FotoFest, 1988, unpaginated.

— . *FotoFest 90: The International Month
of Photography.* Houston: Houston
FotoFest, 1990, 128–29.

— . *Houston FotoFest 1986: The Month of
Photography.* Houston: Houston FotoFest,
1986, unpaginated.

Houston Women's Caucus for Art. *Self
Images: The 1985 Show.* Houston: Houston
Women's Caucus for Art, 1985, 22.

Landay, Janet, and Donald Barthelme.
*One + One: Collaborations by Artists and
Writers.* Houston: Glassell School of Art,
Museum of Fine Arts, Houston, 1988, 24–26,
36, 41.

Lyons, Nathan, ed. *Photography in the 20th
Century.* New York: Horizon Press, 1967,
119.

— , ed. *Photography 63/An International
Exhibition.* Rochester, N.Y.: George
Eastman House, 1963, 49.

Merlo, Lorenzo. *Swimming Pools.*
Amsterdam: St. Canon Photo Gallery, 1986.

Nodal, Al. *Texas Photo Sampler.*
Washington, D.C.: Washington Project for
the Arts, 1981.

Perloff, Stephen. *Philadelphia: Past and
Present.* Philadelphia: Philadelphia Art
Alliance, 1982.

Philadelphia Museum of Art. *Philadelphia:
Three Centuries of American Art.* Philadelphia: Philadelphia Museum of Art, 1976,
586.

Pocock, Philip J. *Exposition internationale
de photographie: Regards sur la terre des
hommes* (The Camera as Witness).
Montreal: Expo 67, 1967, image 34.

Rice, Shelly, ed. *Past and Present: Photography Faculty, Bucks County Community
College.* Newton, Pa.: Hicks Art Center
Gallery, Bucks County Community College,
1983, unpaginated.

Stein, Judith. *George Krause: 1960–1981.*
Philadelphia: Morris Gallery, Pennsylvania
Academy of Fine Arts, 1981.

Szarkowski, John. *Mirrors and Windows:
American Photography Since 1960.* New
York: Museum of Modern Art, 1978, 37.

— . Introduction to *New Photography USA.*
London: Photographers' Gallery, 1972.

— . Introduction to *Photographie nouvelle
des Etats-Unis.* New York: Museum of
Modern Art; Paris: Bibliothèque Nationale,
1971, 12–13.

— . *The Photographer's Eye.* New York:
Museum of Modern Art, 1966, 68.

Torino Fotografia Biennale Internazionale.
Torino Fotografia 85. Turin, Italy:
AIDEL-Torino Fotografia, 1985, 77–80.

— . *Torino Fotografia 87.* Turin, Italy:
AIDEL-Torino Fotografia, 1987, 147.

Tucker, Anne W., ed. *The Anthony G.
Cronin Memorial Collection: The Museum of
Fine Arts, Houston.* Houston: Museum of
Fine Arts, Houston, unpaginated.

— . "George Krause." In *AIPAD '84:
Fifth Annual Exposition.* New York:
AIPAD, 1984.

Venice Photographic Biennial. *Venezia
'79—La fotografia.* Milan: Electa, 1979.

Wainwright, Nicholas B., ed. *Sculpture of a
City: Philadelphia's Treasures in Bronze
and Stone.* New York: Walker Publishing
Company, 1974.

Yale University Art Gallery. *Photography
in America 1850–1965.* New Haven, Conn.:
Yale University Art Gallery, 1965, image 71.

Selected Articles and Reviews

Auer, James. "Gallery Gazing: Shows
in Review." *Milwaukee Journal,*
2 November 1975.

Art in America. "Young Talent USA,"
June 1963, 46–57.

Bowles, D. "Lone Star Tapestry." *Artweek*
12 (7 November 1981): 12.

Burke, Paul. "Grande Dame of the Gulf."
Texas Monthly, December 1983, 160–69,
216–26.

*Camera: International Magazine for Pho-
tography.* "Photography, A Contemporary
Compendium: Second Part," December
1975, 29, 43.

Camera 35. "First Time on View: World's
Greatest Picture Collection." 8 (August–
September 1964): 26, 54.

Carli-Ballola, Giampiero. "A tu per tu con i maestri." *Il fotografo*, September 1979, 36–37.

Cava, Paul, and M. E. Mankus. "Interview with George Krause." *Philadelphia Arts Exchange*, January 1977.

Clever, L. A. "George Krause." *Siren* (Houston), March 1991, cover, inside cover, 7.

Clichés (Brussels). "À propos du voyeurisme," June 1988, 32–39.

Coleman, A.D. "Latent Image: Death as a Living Reality." *Village Voice*, 13 July 1972.

Colombo, Attilio. "Interviste con i responsabli." *Progresso fotografico*, no. 7–8 (July–August 1979): 34–36.

Connoisseur (London). Review of "Mirrors and Windows" exhibition at the City Art Center, Edinburgh (August 1981): 244–45.

Crossley, Mimi. "Capturing Krause." *Houston Post Spotlight*, 10 October 1976.

— . "Houston's first whole look at work of photographer who out-classicizes the cool ones." *Houston Post*, 19 February 1978.

— . "Reviews: Michael Rummery, George Krause." *Houston Chronicle*, 7 November 1980.

Daho, Sergio. "Un americano ai confini della fantasia." *Il fotografo*, November 1979, 40–47.

Day, Chapin. "City Clicks: Philadelphia Begins to Recognize Photography as Art." *Philadelphia Inquirer*, 10 February 1975.

Deschin, Jacob. "Five Show at Modern: Group Photo Exhibit Points Up Differences." *New York Times*, 2 June 1963.

DeShazo, Edith. "George Krause and Minor White Exhibit Photos." *Philadelphia Inquirer*, 4 May 1976.

Donohoe, Victoria. "Photography: Art or Eyewash?" *Philadelphia Inquirer*, 12 January 1969.

Dressman, Fran. "Artists' Awards Show UH Focus of Houston Art Scene." *Horizons* (University of Houston), Fall 1986, 4–5.

— . "Balancing Images and Words." *Horizons* (University of Houston), February 1988, 6.

Eletti, Valerio. "La galleria dell'immagine: Mostre e convegni: Roma: George Krause all'Accademia Americana." *Il diaframma*, no. 249 (April–May 1980): 29–30.

El nacional (Caracas). "Fotografías de George Krause inauguran mañana en el museo," 9 August 1969; "Las fotografías de Krause," 11 August 1969.

Ennis, Michael. "The Elegiac Image." *Texas Monthly*, August 1982, 138–42.

Everingham, Carol J. "After 144 Years 'Photography as Art' is Still an Aesthetic Issue." *Houston Arts Magazine*, February 1983, 11.

Forman, Nessa. "Krause: Technical Eye, Sensitive Heart." *Philadelphia Bulletin*, 24 January 1982.

Foto (Netherlands). "Houston FotoFest '88," June 1988, 86.

Fotografie 78. "Knihy." Review of *George Krause 1*, by George Krause, 1978, 78.

Harper's Bazaar. "The Editor's Guest Book," December 1968, 91, 93, 115, 124, 157.

Hellebrand, Nancy. "I Nudi: George Krause." *Philadelphia Photo Review* 5, no. 4 (Summer 1981): 6–7.

Hill, Ed. "Lone Star Photographer." *Southwest Media Review* 2 (Spring 1983): 9–14.

Houston Chronicle. "Campus Chancellor Vetoes Nude Student Photos in UH Yearbook," 14 July 1978; "UH Panel Supports Inclusion of Nude Photos in Annual," 8 July 1976.

Houston Chronicle Southwest Guide to Living. "Exhibition of George Krause Photographs Focuses Upon Shrines, Nudes," 15 February 1978.

Houston Metropolitan, August 1989, 59.

Houston Post. "Booklets of Nude Photos Being Given Away on UH Campus," 10 April 1981.

Infinity: American Society of Magazine Photographers. "George Krause," November 1965, cover, 18–25.

Jarmusch, Ann. "What Makes a Photograph Great?" *Philadelphia Inquirer*, 14 March 1976.

Jenkins, Peggy. "Profile: George Krause." *Contact Sheet* (Allen Street Gallery, Dallas) 11, no. 4 (Fall 1987): 3, 4.

Jensen, Dean. "Shutterbugs Learn to Snap Form Divine." *Milwaukee Sentinel*, 31

March 1982.

Jiménez, Oscar Rojas. "George Krause y escuela de Caracas en el Museo de Bellas Artes." *El universal* (Caracas), 7 April 1974.

Johnson, Patricia. "The Artist: George Krause's Photographic Work is More Dream Images Than Reality and Speaks Directly to the Viewer." *Houston Chronicle Zest Magazine*, 5 August 1984.

Kalil, Susie. "Works by MacConnel, Krause, Nakian and Hoover." *Houston Post*, 14 November 1982.

Kalina, Judith Schoener. "George Krause." *Camera 35* 20, no.9 (December 1976): 52–57, 59.

Katz, Jonathan G. "Around the Galleries: Irreverent nudes from a native son." *Philadelphia Bulletin*, (day?) April 1981.

Krause, George. "The Naked Truth." *Image* (Houston Center for Photography) 2 (September 1983): 18–19.

— . "Tools of the Art: Paper Tiger." *Camera Arts* 1, no. 2 (March–April 1981): 94–95.

— . "And We Have Come to Know All Places: A Photographic Essay." *Harper's Bazaar*, April 1963, 164–67.

Krueger, Joline Gutierrez. "Arts: Krause Photographs Bits of Humanity." *Daily Lobo* (University of N. Mex., Albuquerque), 6 April 1987.

Kutner, Janet. "Krause Turns Photos Into Surrealistic Art." *Dallas Morning News*, 30 September 1976.

Life Magazine. "Gallery: Boy in Waterfall," 23 October 1970, 6–7.

Life Special Edition: The World of Children. "New Born." *Life Magazine*, Spring 1990, 28–31.

Life Thirtieth Anniversary Issue on Photography. "The Power of Seeing," 23 December 1966, 133–54.

Maddox, Jerald. "Creative Photography 1869–1969." *Quarterly Journal of the Library of Congress*, January 1971, 24, 27.

McFarland, Gay Elliott. "Work Home, George Krause: Looking at Life Through a Lens." *Houston Chronicle*, 7 November 1980.

McLanahan, Lynn. "Photography in Houston." *Artspace* 7 (Spring 1983): 30–33.

Meline, Caroline. "Photographer Wins Global Plaudits, but His Heart's in Phila." *Philadelphia Inquirer*, 15 January 1982.

Muchnic, Suzanne. "Galleries: West Los Angeles." *Los Angeles Times*, 27 November 1981.

Newhall, Beaumont. "Reality/USA." *Art in America* 52, no. 6 (December 1964): 90–96.

Novak, Alan. "Krause Show at Afterimage." *Dallas Morning News Weekend Guide*, 8 October 1976.

Pantalone, John. "Photos with the Strength and Spirit of Life." *Newport: This Week* (Salve Regina College), 18 October 1984.

Peuloff, Stephen. "Death and Transformation." *Philadelphia Photo Review* 1, no. 5

(May 1976): 6–8.

Philadelphia Photo Review. "Mancini Publishes Krause Catalogue and Poster," Winter 1981, 11.

Polak, Maralyn Lois. "Interview: George Krause, 'My Business is to Search Out Images.'" *Philadelphia Inquirer*, 6 June 1975.

Popular Photography's Invitation to Photography, Spring 1975, 70.

Porter, Allan. "Malagueña, a Photographic Essay by George Krause." *Camera: International Magazine for Photography* 45 (January 1966): 4–15.

Power, Mark. "George Krause: A Quiet Intensity." *Lightwork*, November 1974, 10–16.

Print. "Best U.S. Posters of the Decade," July–August 1971, 36, 60.

Renegade Rip (Bakersfield College, Calif.), 20 February 1990, 5 March 1990.

Richard, Paul. "Between the Stripes." *Washington Post*, 26 February 1983.

Robinson, Joan Seeman. Review of Harris Gallery exhibition. *Artforum* 28, no. 10 (Summer 1990): 171–72.

Rocky Mountain News. "Eye on Art: Which Qualities Make Photos Memorable?" 28 November 1980.

Salgado, Robert J. "Get the Picture: Classes for Would-Be Photographers." *Philadelphia Inquirer*, 5 October 1969.

— . "How to Select Photos for an

Exhibition." *Philadelphia Bulletin*,
12 January 1979.

Scarborough, John. "A New Resident Artist
at UH: Photographer Balances Teaching,
Creative Work." *Houston Chronicle*,
3 September 1975.

— . "George Krause Six-Hour Photography
Workshop Fills Void." *Houston Chronicle*,
5 November 1980.

— . "Krause Exhibit Shows Growth in
Artist's Work." *Houston Chronicle*,
8 November 1980.

— . "Krause Show Here is Fertile and
Unconventional." *Houston Chronicle*,
13 October 1976.

Schwartz, Rhona, and Paul Moraus. "Con-
troversy Surprises Art Prof." *Daily Cougar*
(University of Houston), 12 July 1978.

Setzer, Ruth. "A Close Look at the 'Sculpture of a City.'" *Philadelphia Inquirer*,
14 November 1974.

Shirey, David. "Making the Rounds of Photo
Shows." *New York Times*, 1 July 1972.

Shulte, Rainer, ed. *Translation Review*
(University of Tex. at Dallas) 30 (1989): cover.

Sigala, José. "Fotografías 1 George Krause."
Papelos (Caracas) 9 (September 1969): 73–87.

Smith, Debby. "Photographer's Art Steps
into Another World." *Abilene Reporter-News*
(Tex.), 27 May 1978.

Southwest Art. "George Krause," February
1990, 168.

Stevens, Carol. "Saints, Martyrs and
Everyday Mysteries." *Print* 24, no. 6
(November–December 1970): 44–51.

Stevens, Nancy. "Gallery: I Nudi." *American Photographer* 6, no. 4 (April 1981): 22.

Szarkowski, John. "The Art of Photography:
A Contradiction in Terms?" *Film and Photography: A Newsweek Global Report*,
7 October 1968, 4–7.

35mm Photography. "Gallery 35," Winter
1973, 86–89.

Thornton, Gene. "Inanimate, But Full of
Life." *New York Times*, 9 July 1972.

Tucker, Anne W. "A Vision Bound by
Diversity." *American Photographer*
18 (May 1987): 67–75.

—. "The Evocative Presence." *Bulletin
of the Museum of Fine Arts, Houston*,
Winter–Spring 1988, 54.

Tucker, Anne W., and John Scarborough.
"Contemporary Photography in Houston."
Artspace 1 (Summer 1977): 4–9.

Valdez, Carmen Teresa. "En el Museo de
Bellas Artes." *El universal*, 8 April 1974.

Weiss, Murray. "Introduction: Two Young
Philadelphians, Don Donaghy and George
Krause." *Contemporary Photographer*,
Fall 1962.

Selected Collections

Addison Gallery of American Art,
Andover, Mass.

Amon Carter Museum, Fort Worth, Tex.

Anthony G. Cronin Memorial Collection,
Museum of Fine Arts, Houston

Art Institute of Chicago

Bibliothèque Nationale, Paris

Carpenter Center for the Visual Arts, Harvard
University, Cambridge

Center for Creative Photography, University
of Arizona, Tucson

Chrysler Museum, Norfolk, Va.

FotoFest 90 International Laser Videodisc
Library, Houston

George Eastman House, Rochester, N.Y.

Gernsheim Collection, University of Texas at
Austin

Library of Congress, Washington, D.C.

Museo de Bellas Artes, Caracas

Museum of Fine Arts, American Academy
in Rome

Museum of Fine Arts, Boston

Museum of Fine Arts, Houston

Museum of Fine Arts, New Orleans

Museum of Modern Art, New York

National Museum of American Art,
Smithsonian Institution, Washington, D.C.

Philadelphia Museum of Art

Worcester Art Museum, Mass.

Captions